Praise for Martin Kihn's

BAD DOG

"The most touching, original buddy story I've come across in ages. Sit. Stay. Read." —Walter Kirn, author of *Up in the Air*

"This sharply written, darkly funny memoir-cum-dog story-cum-recovery tale is a quick, absorbing read that will serve a wide audience well."
—*Library Journal* (starred review)

"[A] wry memoir of the human-dog bond. . . . Raw, deeply sincere, and self-aware."
—*Publishers Weekly* (starred review)

"Will knock you over and charm you, all while licking your face." —Charles Yu, author of *How to Live Safely in a Science Fictional Universe*

"A modern masterpiece that captures the dark side of K9 love." —Dogster.com

Martin Kihn

BAD DOG

Martin Kihn is an Emmy Award–nominated former writer for MTV's *Pop-Up Video* and the author of *House of Lies* and *A$$hole*. He has worked at *Spy*, *Forbes*, and *New York*, and his articles have appeared in *The New York Times*, *GQ*, *Details*, and *Cosmopolitan*. He lives in Minneapolis.

www.martykihn.com

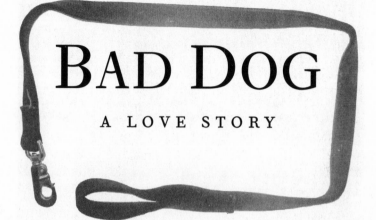

BAD DOG

A LOVE STORY

Martin Kihn

Vintage Books

A DIVISION OF RANDOM HOUSE, INC.

NEW YORK

FIRST VINTAGE BOOKS EDITION, APRIL 2012

Copyright © 2011 by Martin Kihn

The Library of Congress has cataloged the Pantheon edition as follows:
Kihn, Martin
Bad dog : a love story / Martin Kihn.
p. cm.
1. Dogs—New York (State)—New York—Anecdotes.
2. Bernese mountain dogs—New York (State)—New York—Anecdotes.
3. Bernese mountain dogs—Behavior—New York (State)—New York—Anecdotes.
4. Dog Owners—New York (State)—New York—Anecdotes.
5. Human-animal relationship—New York (State)—New York—Anecdotes.
6. Kihn, Martin. I. Title.
SF426.2.K49 2011
636.70092'9
2010035355

Vintage ISBN: 978-0-307-47746-0

Book design by Robert C. Olsson

www.vintagebooks.com

Printed in the United States of America
10 9 8 7 6 5 4 3 2 1

There's a book to be written on Zen and the art of dog train-ing. Training requires total concentration. If you're not all there, neither is your dog. If you're jumpy, so is your dog.

—Susan Conant, *A New Leash on Death*

To love and admire anything outside yourself is to take one step away from utter spiritual ruin.

—C. S. Lewis

The American Kennel Club started its Canine Good Citizen certification program in 1989 to encourage dogs and their companions to be better members of society. To get certified, a dog must pass ten tests of obedience, good manners, and grooming. The AKC considers these ten tests to be "only the beginning," but anyone who has ever loved a dog may have another word for them.

Impossible.

And I don't mean for the dog.

Bad Dog

Entering the Ring

"Is it just me," I ask my ninety-pound copilot, framed in the rearview mirror like a hairy Warhol Marilyn, "or is everyone losing their minds?"

I'm sorry to say, she seems to be sorry to say, *it's just you.*

"Did we miss our turn? I can't see the signs."

And I, she says, *can't read.*

Now I will advise that when you're going somewhere that is not so easy to get to, don't let me drive.

There are few guarantees in life like the one I will make to you now: you will get lost. Very lost. So far from your destination you'll be looking out the window as darkness descends, watching street signs change into another language. During my days as the world's most ungrateful management consultant, I tooled around London in a rented Ford Fiesta with one of the firm's partners, who spun on me after a string of boneheaded turns and said, "Who was it that hired you again?"

Losing her religion, my copilot—a five-year-old Bernese mountain dog named Hola—stretches herself out on the backseat of our alarmingly small car and moans softly, serenely, like a butterfly being sawn in half by wind.

"You're not helping," I say to her, as the Sprain Brook Parkway is glazed with a silver coat of fear.

Neither are you. Did you bring any cheese?

"If you're driving," says the guy on 1010 WINS news radio, "think about getting off the road. We have a severe weather warning. It's going to get ugly out there."

Not as ugly as White Plains, New York.

A gray blanket stuffed with old malls, it claims to be thirty minutes north of Manhattan. Ninety minutes after setting out, Hola and I finally slide into the parking lot of the Port Chester Obedience Training Club, where we're scheduled to take the Canine Good Citizen test ten minutes ago.

The PCOTC is a legendary facility that relocated from Port Chester to an industrial district in White Plains without changing its name. It readies little woofers and their handlers for everything from crate training to all-breed shows, and five years earlier, Hola had the distinction of being the only dog in her puppy kindergarten class to be invited to leave. Twice.

Let it not be said that my dog is not a legend in the canine obedience world.

She's a beautiful, tricolored purebred dog; a spectacularly fluffy, optimistic creature with true Broadway spirit and an explosive commitment to now.

I keep expecting her to stand up on her hind paws to make her Tony acceptance speech:

"I remember when I was a little puppy, lying on my doggie bed watching *Beethoven's 3rd* on DVD and thinking, 'I can do that!' . . ."

And I mean no disrespect to her when I say that all things considered, taking the long view and giving her the full benefit of the doubt, she was a horrible bitch.

Storm clouds morph from a hazy gray to an oily, ominous rust as the volume of snow per square inch of air throttles up.

"Hola, come!" I say, holding open the car's back door.

Because I have enough cut-up raw liver in my snow jacket pocket to open a meat market, she jumps out.

I saddle her into her little harness, lock the car, check that I have her dog license, rabies tag, hairbrush, and—the critical item—her complete attention. Then I tuck myself into classic dog handler's heeling position, left arm bent with my hand on my sacral third chakra, body erect and as still as the truth.

Stepping off on my left foot, cuing Hola to heel, I start toward our destiny.

Miraculously, she follows.

Step, step. Head up. Sky down. My jeans feeling loose on my stress-addled torso, I can finally exhale.

We skate the iron ramp, negotiate past a boxer puppy in the outer swing doors, and I ask Hola to sit in front of the second set of doors so I can precede her.

Always lead, you see: follow a dog and you follow a doubt.

"Hola, sit."

Remember: name first, command second.

I say: "*Grrr.*"

Aversive sound, meaning: Seriously, sit.

Hola sits.

As I pull the door open, seeing the ring set up for the test, with the white PVC accordion gates, the official note takers and stewards, the distracter dog for the dreaded item #8 (reaction to another dog), a dozen or so of our training buddies nervously clamped to the walls watching the empty ring, the evaluator pacing the expanse of Mity-Lite polymer matting looking for stray treats left over from Family Manners class, the industrial warehouse roofing and the rusted crates and agility equipment strewn like an A-frame junkyard in the far ring, the beautiful goldens and Labs and Havanese stress-smiling in a united chorus of *Hello, world!*—well, we have only one thought, Hola and me.

We are home.

Release word: "Okay."

She trails me into the club.

What we're doing here is a canine mystery.

If you'd told me one year earlier that the two of us could trot into Port Chester as legitimate contenders for an American Kennel Club–sanctioned obedience certification—Canine Good Citizen—I'd have thought you had rolled your brain in catnip and set it on fire.

Begun in 1989, the CGC is a test of training and temperament; to pass, a dog has to be able to sit quietly for petting and around other dogs, tolerate handling and distractions, walk on a loose lead through a crowd, prove it knows basic commands such as sit, down, stay, and come, and endure a few minutes' separation from its owner without obvious distress.

Some dogs can pass it after a couple of classes and a pep talk.

Then there is Hola.

Everybody knew what was wrong with my dog.

I could take her anywhere, and she particularly enjoyed the works of Pixar. Obeying my whispered commands was like breathing to her, and at times I entertained the idea she could actually read my mind. Her sits were so straight you could level a cabinet with them, her down-stays so still they bordered on a trance. Sometimes I'd put her into a stay, go and have a medical procedure, visit my mother in West Virginia, and she'd still be there when I got back from the airport, patiently awaiting my release: "Okay! Good girl."

Not.

Truth was, just one year ago, Hola had never met a word

she could recognize, including her name. Friends and strangers alike were greeted with a full-body slam that was just this side of actionable. The only invitation needed was a smile, a pulse, or a BabyBjörn. My apartment was a wasteland of gnawed dados and wee wee–stained chintz. Walks were a haphazard dance of death as she lunged at any passing Subway wrapper, unleashed Pomeranian, or Crip.

"She doesn't mean to be bad," said one of the trainers my wife and I consulted during Hola's first few years on earth. "She's just kind of high-strung."

There are other words for what she was.

"Why is she always running around and jumping on people and not listening?" I asked the guy, who handled K-9 police dogs.

"That's easy," he said. "You don't know anything about dogs."

Ah.

We'd had so much hope, my wife, Gloria, and I. It still stings me to remember with what prematernal optimism we read Jean Donaldson and Karen Pryor and Sharon Chesnutt Smith's *The New Bernese Mountain Dog*, scouring hardware stores for these strange things called baby gates. She mail-ordered a Bernese-ready version of what dog people call a crate—it's a cage—and I almost had a petit mal. It was bigger than our Toyota Echo.

Dreams die hard, and so did this one. Puppies are a pain at any price, and we marked up a lot to exuberance. Certainly she wasn't shy. Just ask our neighbors. Many times she helped them with their groceries and tossed in a prostate exam on the house. Years passed and passed again.

At a certain point, without announcing it even to ourselves, we gave up. I gave up. We'd had our idea of what a pet should be and had been baited and switched. We'd been had by the dogs of the gods or vice versa. She was housebroken; she seemed happy; she didn't actually bite people, with a single exception.

What I know now is that settling for a dog who is housebroken and doesn't draw blood is like settling for a child who can talk.

And I might as well admit the exception was my wife.

Gradually—very gradually—as we stopped working with Hola, she turned into a beast. There are reasonable people who would have euthanized her for the way she treated Gloria, and to those people I have no response.

"She's a wild one, dude," said another of the trainers we visited to deal with this new reign of terror—the occasional growling, the passing nips, the light bruising and marks on my wife's arms and legs that more than once had a predictable result.

"How'd that happen?" asked some woman at Ann Taylor or at the Whole Foods where Gloria worked for a year as a cook.

"My dog did it."

A look of deep, sisterly karma. "It's okay," they'd whisper. "You don't have to lie for him anymore. There are people who can help you."

"Really, it's my dog. She's a menace."

"Of course it is, girlfriend. Of course it is."

Wink.

Of course it's the man. And were they so wrong? Where was the man, after all?

So I am being sincere when I say I don't lay blame for what Gloria decided to do next. She saved both of our lives—mine and the dog's—after all.

She left us.

Gloria is a wiry, birdlike woman with bobbed brown hair, a sharp nose, and milk-bottle glasses; she's usually smiling slightly as though eavesdropping on a funny conversation. Her eyes are a serious blue that almost glows, and her skin is pale and buttery, her features stacked together with such unusual symmetry that the first thing my male friends usually said to me after meeting her was: "Wow."

A professional charmer, she's reduced vanloads of folk-song fans in Manhattan's East Village to tears with her gorgeous voice, tart lyrics, and improvised monologues. The one about the death of Frank Sinatra was a classic I wish I'd committed to tape. She has a master's in music theory and can recognize any celebrity, no matter how obscure, by their voice.

People love her, and those who do not simply haven't met her yet. She is utterly uncontroversial. Coincidentally, she's suffered a few dog years herself. She'd decided to go to cooking school, worked for a while, and then quit because the career was too dangerous and poorly paid.

Inspired by the old *Schoolhouse Rock* series, she started writing one-minute songs about cooking techniques—"Read the Recipe All the Way Through"; "Shock-Shock-Shock the Vegetables," in the style of the Ramones; the ribald "Pull Wiggle Wiggle," a pseudo-gospel song about how to bone a fish—and set them to animated videos featuring a trio of musical chefs named Do, Re, and Mi.

Chefdoremi.com is her message to the world, which so far is considering its response.

I still believe she is some kind of genius, but she has reservations.

And, like many Gen Xers, we'd sort of forgotten to have children until it was probably too late.

As snow continues to swallow the obedience club, I hand back the CGC forms in triplicate. AKC registration number—yes.

Spayed—yes. Age—almost six now, an old lady in Bernese mountain dog time.

"You'll be second," says the steward. "Wait over at the side, please."

Let's go into the corner, Hola seems to say, *and remind me what I'm supposed to do here. Preferably using a food lure.*

As I'm walking backward monitoring Hola's stay, I scan the ring where the first team is doing item #7, "Coming when called."

The dog half of the pair is a rather sluggish toy poodle who meanders back to her handler like she's waist-deep in canola oil.

"Did you see that, Hola?" I whisper. "No pizzazz at all."

That poodle lacks heart, she agrees. *She has no business out there on the mat.*

For the first ten years of my marriage, after a month locked in a rehab I don't remember checking into, I'd been abstinent from alcohol.

Stop me if you've heard this story before.

Burned out as a TV writer, I went back to business school and got a job as a management consultant, working out of hotel rooms in cities far, far away, and one night I went into the mini-bar for a Diet Pepsi and thought, *Well, nothing livens up a Diet Pepsi like some Captain Morgan, correct?*

So I took out the bottle and unscrewed the cap.

I see now the difference between sobriety and abstinence is like the difference between marriage and pornography. It's apples and rotary saws.

To her credit, Gloria stayed with me through my bottom, stayed with Hola and me as we began our own *Incredible Journey* of mutual rehabilitation, then went off on a journey of her own.

To this day, I understand.

In the words of a country song she wrote, "You're Leavin' Me, You Lucky Dog (If I Was You I'd Leave Me Too)."

Hola and I trotted on alone: to a terrifying dog camp in the Green Mountains of Virginia, a gallery of trainers and priests, all-breed shows, and obedience demonstrations, meeting wonderful people along the way—the top Bernese mountain dog breeder, the national canine obedience champion, the world's best dog writer, even the head of the CGC program herself.

It doesn't take an advanced degree in animal behavior to see that I traded an obsession with alcohol for an obsession with dog training.

But looking back, I like to give our adventure a more romantic spin: we were trying to get Gloria back. Somehow I thought succeeding in the impossible task of winning our four-legged demon child a Canine Good Citizen rating would make us both family friendly again.

To be fair, Gloria didn't know this; even I didn't know this in the beginning.

But I'm sure that Hola did.

We're practicing our automatic sits as the steward comes up to us from the judge's table.

She's a large, older woman in an L.L. Bean red flannel shirt, and her breath spreads out in front of her like a paint roller. Her wide face is a map of White Plains: gray, flat, and functional.

"Are you Hola?" she asks me.

"Yes."

"Here for the CGC, right? Not Therapy Dog?"

"Yes."

"You're up next. Use the buckle collar. Leave the treats outside the ring. Are you ready?"

I peer down at my sidekick, whose head is cocked to the left quizzically in a look that says life is a punch line, so you'd better be joking.

"Are we ready, girlfriend?"

Are you kidding me? she says, breaking her sit on my cue. *I was BORN ready!*

So we enter the ring . . .

CHAPTER ONE

The Purebred

IF YOU WANT to get a purebred dog, all I can say is good luck. Almost by definition, you won't get a good one, not if you're a civilian who lives in that sad world outside the show rings. Purebreds are graded in degrees of conformation to an ideal standard—the perfect specimen. That's what judges are doing at Westminster or in the movie *Best in Show*: sizing up against the standard, some combination of physics and temperament that the AKC has written down but good judges know in their heart.

Very Platonic. And just as in Plato's *Republic*, the further you get from this ideal expression, the closer you get to your life.

Dog breeders have a term for this kind of life—the kind you'll get if you're blessed enough to get anything at all. It's called "pet quality." And in the world of purebred dogs, pet quality is not who you want dating your daughter.

Gloria had always wanted a dog. She'd grown up with a St. Bernard, a big dumb animal named Alex who'd missed the critical socialization window and didn't play well with others. But he adored Gloria, as we all do, and set her on the path to large dogs.

I'd been tempted by the Bernese myself a few times. As my ex-sister-in-law once said, "They're the George Clooney of dogs." The word is *charm*. Even though I didn't like woofies, I was lured along a train platform in Bennington, Vermont, by a Bernese male who smiled at me, ambled between my legs, and flopped onto the ground with that full-throated yogic breath release I've come to know so well. It's like they're exhaling all the bad vibrations in the world.

The owner was a rambling, friendly guy with about a hundred kids, and my wife got to asking him what the dogs were like.

"Let's just say," he said, "you have to include them. They don't like to be left out."

Color me similar.

Gloria claims she got my permission to look for a Bernese of our own. I was still swimming in moonshine at this point, which didn't help my memory, but I'd hate to think she took advantage of this for her own schemes. She told me later she just wanted a friend in the house for a change. I was home with my wife very rarely, even when I was home with my wife, if you get what I mean.

"I want a puppy," she supposedly said.

"That's okay by me," I theoretically answered. "What kind?"

"A Bernese mountain dog. They're very sweet."

"As big as that one in Vermont?"

"Oh, no," she lied to my face. "The females are much smaller."

"Okey dokey," I hypothetically concluded, cracking open another Mickey's Wide Mouth.

At the time I shared the prejudice—common to co-op boards, landlords, and other fools the world over—that smaller dogs are somehow more domesticated. Nothing could be further from the truth. Big dogs might seem like more trouble, but they tend to be lazy and fat. Small dogs are like the most annoying runt you ever knew in high school, plus fangs.

As their name implies, purebreds tend to come from breeders, and breeders are a class apart. When it comes to deciding who is worthy of their spawn, the best ones are as selective as the Harvard Admissions Committee. More selective, actually—Harvard doesn't do home inspections.

"How's it going?" I'd ask Gloria by phone from the Marriott, watching the Mondavi swoosh against the bathroom water glass.

"Not too good," she'd say.

"What's the problem this time? We don't know Dick Cheney? We're not on *American Idol*?"

"It's the yard. We don't have a fenced-in yard."

"We live in the New York area, for fuck's sake. Nobody has a yard."

"And we never had a Bernese before. That's a problem, too."

"First time for everything," I fumed. "What're we, supposed to get our dog from a pet store?"

Sick silence as we thought about where pet store puppies come from. If you haven't heard of puppy mills I won't kill your buzz by describing them. Just imagine the saddest song you've ever heard and add barking.

"I don't know," she said. "The last one made me fill out this four-page application and give references. I had to swear to feed the dog organic liver. We had an easier time getting the mortgage."

"What's so great about this dog anyway? It's just a stupid pet."

"I have to go," said my wife. "The other phone's ringing."

It was only after she hung up I remembered we didn't have another phone.

Eventually, she did find a breeder up in Rochester who agreed to part with a precious pet-quality Bernese for two thousand dollars. That this breeder was not in the first rank was confirmed a few years later when I mentioned her name to one of the champion Berner owners backstage at the Westminster Dog Show in Madison Square Garden.

Pursed lips. "You have to be careful," she said.

But still, it wasn't a puppy mill and it's not like we had options.

My approach to marriage has been to give myself one *no* per year, whether I need it or not. That's how I show who's in charge. I was this close to hauling out that *no* after we wandered into the kitchen of the breeder's roomy suburban ranch house and I heard a loud *thump!* and saw an abominable snowman slam against the back screen door—closed, mercifully—stretching its massive paws six feet in the air as it tried to smash the door in and go about its evil work.

I think I actually yelped and grabbed Gloria. Then the breeder woman appeared from somewhere and did about the single stupidest thing I've ever seen anyone do.

She opened the door.

Yeti hopped onto all fours, trotted directly over to me, smiled, lay down, and rolled onto his back, bicycling his big white paws in the air.

The sole reason I hadn't snagged my wife and bolted for the New York State Thruway was that I had been paralyzed by fear.

"Aw, come on," said the breeder, whose name was Florence.

"W-what?" I shuddered.

"Rub the tummy! Rub the tummy."

I'd get used to the high-pitched Japanese-department-store-girl tone people used with dogs around the time I started doing it myself.

"You have got to be kidding me," I said.

"Aw, he's friendly," squealed Gloria, who was already down next to the grizzly and running her hands through the thick white curls on his barrel belly. "*Who wants the tummy rub! Who wants the tummy rub.*"

Dog people tend to repeat themselves, because they don't have much to say.

By this time four or five marginally smaller specimens had appeared and were milling around the kitchen and conspiring to knock me off my feet. Figuring it was safer to lower my center of gravity, I crouched down next to Gloria and touched the beast.

"That's Bella," said Florence. "He's the sire. I flew him in from Switzerland."

"What does he weigh?" I asked.

"Oh, hardly anything. One twenty or so. He's lost weight. What a doll. These others are bitches. They're all mine."

As I was contemplating how casually dog people throw around that word *bitch,* one of the creatures collapsed next to Bella and lay there, barely blinking. She was the single tiredest-looking thing with a pulse I'd ever seen in my life.

"Is she sick?" Gloria asked.

"That's the mother. She's exhausted. There's six in the litter."

Moment of silence. The Miracle of Birth. Zzzz.

Bernese mountain dogs are gorgeous animals, as you know, and a big part of that sex appeal comes from their tricolored coat. The fur on Bella's chest and underside was downy and snow white, like the tip of his tail and the blaze on his muzzle. The rest of his thick fur was shiny jet black, with some patches of rust on his cheeks and forelegs. Bernese people think they see on their dogs' chests an inverted Swiss cross, but like the Shroud of Turin it's visible only to believers.

Bella certainly seemed friendly enough. Our strengths are our weaknesses. Bernese err by going overboard.

In retrospect I see that breeder played me like a game of fetch.

We were filling out all the forms that said basically this dog is incredibly special and deserves first-class treatment, and by the way, it's so deeply flawed it must never be allowed to breed. We also said we'd never give the dog away, get it a haircut, feed it Alpo or Mighty Dog or just about anything else, let it skip puppy class or take mind-altering drugs, become a Jehovah's Witness or join the Screen Actors Guild. You only think I'm exaggerating.

Secretly, I kept looking for the xeroxed sheet that said, *P.S. I'm joking, and so is your wife. Ha!*

Although momentarily distracted from my mission by Bella, I can admit to you now I'd decided these forms were not enforceable in human courts and was formulating my speech to Gloria on the way back to the city—*You know, dear, it's not you or the dog; it's me, but . . .*—when Florence unleashed the shock and awe of the unscrupulous breeder. Casually, she said:

"Oh, do you want to see the puppies?"

"No," I said.

She led us into the back room, where there was a kind of corral made of busted cardboard boxes and newspaper and a big bowl of water. And six little five-week-old cute-attacks waiting to happen.

If you haven't seen a baby Bernese mountain dog, spare yourself. They have a way of separating a fool from his senses.

"Do you want to hold one?" Florence asked me.

"No."

She picked up a particularly roly-poly, docile example of the breed and instructed me to cradle him in my left hand close to my body and run my other hand down his little fuzzy body. He all but purred.

"Cute, huh."

It wasn't a question.

Out of the corner of my eye, down in the puppy corral, I noticed one of the litter careening around like a nutcase, kicking newspaper out of the way, trying to chew a hole in the back wall, and doing a Mexican hat dance with her hind legs.

Gosh, I remember thinking, *what's wrong with that one?*

What's wrong was that three weeks later, when we drove back to Rochester, that was the one we took home.

My Scottish mother experienced the Miracle of Birth three times and claims she could tell right from the beginning what we would be like when we were older.

"Your brother was a wonderful baby," she told me many times. "Very calm and in control. I knew he'd be special." Gag.

"Your sister was a fighter, right away. She scrambled for everything. She's still quite, uh, insistent on her point of view."

"What about me?" I asked her, begging for a beating.

"Well," she said, looking plaintive and misty, like one of her favorite sheep had choked on some haggis. "I won't lie," she lied. "You were a difficult child. Always sensitive and moody. It was hard to keep you interested. I think you had that ADD. And you decided you didn't need your mother. It was like you didn't trust me to take care of you."

Most breeders claim that a dog has a basic personality from the start, called a temperament, and they try to match it with the prospective owner. Want a dog to do work on the farm? A serious disposition with good focus, high drive—check. Want a dog to bring you the remote and lie in your lap during *Nick at Nite*? Placid, not too smart, unambitious—check. Want a dog you can bring to nursing homes as a therapy dog? Smart, submissive, not easily startled—check.

Want a dog that is naturally dominant, feels no pain, is as outgoing as Ethel Merman on Jolt and is orally fixated? Say *hola* to Hola. The dog for the couple so ignorant they didn't even know to ask for the results of the puppy temperament test. Good breeders do this test at around seven weeks, and it involves a few simple probes, like putting the puppy on her back, making a sharp noise, setting her down, and walking away—tests for dominance (bad), sensitivity (good), and friendliness (super).

Florence did the test on Hola. I saw the sheets of paper in her hand. For some strange reason, she was reluctant to let us get a look at them.

"She'll make a great therapy dog," she said. "She's got a great temperament."

Unless that woman was practicing her stand-up comedy act, she is going to Hell.

But no matter. I'm grateful for our lack of knowledge, in a way. The other buyers were obviously more savvy than we were—they didn't get Hola, after all—but if we'd known better, we wouldn't have taken her. We'd have seen the red flags. Then where would she go?

The ride back to the city was complicated by the fact that Rochester was frosted by ice from a massive storm that had left its suburbs dark at noon. Florence had a generator, or we wouldn't have been able to see the puppies. It took eight hours to get home, and Hola squirmed and cried in my lap in the passenger's seat until I stumbled on a strange way to shut her up.

The Purebred

The trouble begins.

Three words: Christian contemporary radio.

Put her out like a Christmas light.

"I know this seems like a mistake," I said to Gloria as we skirted around Ithaca. "But I want you to know, I feel in my heart this was a good idea."

I'm not sure what made me so sure, so sincere. It was out of character. But I meant it. Hola was peaceful now, the Christians were singing, the ice storm was behind us, and our family's average attractiveness level had just doubled.

I didn't even think about a drink until we ran into some traffic on the Henry Hudson Bridge.

CHAPTER TWO

The Puppy

WHEN YOU'RE BUYING A DOG, you're buying a tragedy. But when you're buying an Hola, you're buying a farce.

That first night she cried herself to sleep, and frankly so did I. The puppy books had warned us that the transition would be difficult for her—she'd just spent eight weeks lying in a big pile of brothers and sisters and nuzzling her mom, after all. A cold wood floor in the middle of winter next to a couple of un-demonstrative Midwestern white people must have seemed like an anticlimax.

Luckily, dogs have a five-minute memory. Every day is *Groundhog Day*. Next morning, our little bundle greeted the dawn with a big yawn and stretch, started pumping her white-tipped tail like an oar through the river of time, bared all her ivory teeth in what the good-natured would see as a smile, and immediately gave herself a job she would keep during our entire life together: Daddy's wake-up alarm.

From the beginning, if I was in bed and it was dawn some-where in the Western world, Hola was filled with a sense of injustice. She'd whine and wheedle and, if that didn't work, leap onto the bed and start practicing the cha-cha on my chest.

"It's like she wants you to go to work," Gloria said. "Isn't it cute?"

"Cute is not the word."

"Dog food isn't cheap, you know. She's a sensible girl."

"Sensible is not the word."

"Oh, look, she's even breaking in your work shoes for you."

My wife, she left alone. Gloria could sleep until noon and often, frankly, did. But could I catch a couple extra z's on a cold weekend morning when I had no plans and a hangover with a personality? Not in this doggie's lifetime.

Later, I found out it's not uncommon for breeds like the Bernese mountain dog to give themselves a task and execute it faithfully, whether anybody asked them or not. They are part of the working group, a herd of hardy northern breeds like the malamute and Siberian husky that can't guard anything and don't like to fetch. They're muscular, snow-loving animals who don't want to change their minds. Berners were bred by Swiss dairy farmers to haul milk carts to market, so unless they're yanking some dumb jug around town, they just aren't happy.

Since Hola was a morning person, and my wife most definitely was not, the dog and I started every day in a state of culture shock. Not only was she the first dog I ever owned; she was the first dog I ever really knew. If I went over to a friend's apartment or on an outing and there were dogs in the picture, I just stood to one side. They were like a TV commercial that I put on mute.

Of course, it's also true that Gloria and I were Hola's first humans. And despite our Ivy League degrees and theoretically larger forebrains, she found us remarkably easy to train.

It may be possible to make more mistakes with a quadruped than we did, but it wouldn't be easy.

Take the critical task of housebreaking. The number one reason dogs are abandoned to shelters is this bad boy, and we were ready with an action plan. It consisted of us running outside every time Hola squinted, waiting for an hour in the sleet, giving up, and hauling her back inside, only to be treated to a grand production number followed by a TV-ready grin that seemed to say: *Thanks for bringing me back in, guys; I really had to go.*

"This is ridiculous," I said. "That dog can't be trained."

"She's trained all right," said Gloria, ordering yet another carpet online from the Pottery Barn. "We trained her to go on the carpet. Always in that one spot there."

"How'd we do that?"

"I don't know. Maybe it's because you didn't clap that time she went outside." We'd been told you were supposed to treat an outdoor event like the dog just won an Oscar.

"I'm not going to applaud a crap. Listen to yourself."

"All I'm saying is, you're not consistent."

"I'm consistent, all right," I said, popping open another Heinie. "Consistently annoyed. I don't know why we had to get such a big—"

"She's a good girl. She just needs a little help."

At this point our so-called good girl was dipping into a copy of Nora Roberts's *Midnight Bayou*. Very studious. She'd torn off the cover and was working her way through chapter 2. Rarely have I seen someone so thoroughly enjoy a book.

Then there was Hola's campaign to get me to carry her around. Berners aren't always very big. For a couple of months in the beginning of their lives, they're about the size of a watermelon.

Gloria had a name for me. She called me The Holavator.

We lived up two flights of stairs, and when Hola was little I would carry her when she needed to go out. When she got bigger, she expected the same treatment. Every walk with me was a dead stop at the top of the stairs, a plaintive look up at me, and a quick flash of the browns.

As I carried her up and down, she looked around like a little periscope, engaging the wonder of the world. She was happy. On the other hand, as she ballooned in size, I was in danger of needing physical therapy to realign my back. Before long, I had to decommission The Holavator.

By which time she had quietly moved on to stage two of her plan.

Consisting of a subtle shift in her sleeping position. Bernese are peripatetic snoozers, moaning and wandering around all night like they need to police some invisible cows. In the puppy years, since I outsourced things like housebreaking and deworming to my wife and insourced things like snuggling and petting to myself, Hola decided to do most of her wandering around me.

At a certain point, when she was about two years old, she

"Going up?" The Holavator and its passenger.

started hopping onto the bed in the middle of the night and stretching out between us.

Three years later, Gloria still didn't like it: "She really should not be sleeping on the bed."

"Of course not."

"Stop encouraging her."

"I'm not," I protested. "I'm asleep. How am I encouraging her?"

"You smile in your sleep. It's misleading."

Actually, it was Gloria who smiled in her sleep, slightly but unmistakably. I'd always thought it spoke well of her character.

Hola simply waited on the floor beside me, pretending to snore, biding her time. Berners keep their eyes half open when they nap, an odd quirk attributable to double eyelids and an inherited disorder called ectropion, so it was almost impossible to know if she was faking it.

Once Gloria and I were safely sawing wood, Hola pounced onto the bed and started doing something that my better half, of course, took to heart.

"She's rolling up against me," Gloria complained. "It's annoying."

"I think it's cute. She loves you."

"That's not it. I know what she's up to."

"What?"

She looked at me with that semi-exasperated lather I knew so well. "You wouldn't believe me anyway."

"Try me."

A couple nights later, she did. I was in bed drinking an Elephant malt liquor and reading an Agatha Christie; Gloria's eyes were narrow with weariness as she pushed against Hola's supine body with her leg and said: "She's trying to kick me out of the bed. The dog is rolling me onto the floor."

"That's ridiculous. She's just big is all, and she's moving around."

"You're spending more time with her now, and she sees an opening. She's trying to squeeze me out of the picture."

"Oh, come on," I said. "That's silly. She loves you."

"She wants me out of the bed. It's part of her master plan."

"What master plan?"

"She wants to be lady of the house. That little bitch. I know her type. It's like Bonnie Welles in junior high. She's probably up all night pawing in her diary, 'Senator and Mrs. Martin Hola Kihn,' over and over. It's sick."

"You just need some sleep. She's only a dog. They're not that smart."

"Smart enough," said Gloria. "She's smart enough." Then she got a look that I told myself was simply curious:

"How many drinks have you had, Marty?"

"I don't know. Why?"

A moment. "Why don't you try jogging in the mornings? I think you'd like it."

"Sometimes I get the urge to exercise. But I lie down for a while and it goes away."

Ha-ha. I'm here all weekend.

There was always some new suggestion for me—jogging, eating organic, a facial, a colonic. The peanut gallery commented, and I told myself it was almost kind of sweet.

It wasn't sweet. It was a four-alarm fire going on in my house. I heard tears in the night and thought they were a strange, sad dream.

Worry is a prayer for something we don't want to happen. And I was praying all the time. While Gloria cooked and sang and Hola mastered extreme martial arts, I managed to sell my first book. It was written in a white heat early, early in the morning in Marriotts around the world before I started my day as a consultant to drug companies. The firm I worked for pretended to help its clients reach important strategic decisions, and the clients pretended to listen. Days were long, wine a-flowing, the book an exposé that ended my consulting career without replacing it with anything in particular.

But it did get us back onto the island of Manhattan, to a co-op in Washington Heights. I got a job at an online advertising agency with better hours and less travel, Gloria found her way into cooking, and Hola instantly became the acting mayor of the Upper Upper West Side.

A pretty picture all around. A wonderful life.

And then a thousand small doves flew out of a very tall tower.

CHAPTER THREE

The Gates

*Mostly I got loaded quietly, politely. It was something
that took place in my own head.*

—Caroline Knapp,
Drinking: A Love Story

WHICH WAS TRUE.

Except when my head expanded and took over the world.

Take this one story, multiply by ten:

A few years ago, there's a massive art installation in Central
Park, which had been crammed with orange-curtained wooden
structures you could walk through, a momentous exhibit called
The Gates. And it was Saturday, and I was thinking, nice crisp day
in early spring, birds are a-chirp. And it's early as I walk Hola
around the New York–Presbyterian Hospital to visit all her doc-
tor and nurse friends. She'd always been admired by the medical
community because they appreciate expensive luxury goods.

And we're back, and I was drinking my coffee and thinking,
Hey, it's the weekend. There's no reason why not. And somehow I
was in the bathroom sucking on a half-pint bottle of vodka. It
was eight a.m.

And I sat for hours staring at the airshaft, talking to my dog.
Who, for once, wasn't really in the mood.

Topping it off, doing my thing. Four hours later Gloria was
up, and I was saying, Isn't there that orange thing in the park?

The Gates.

She was not a morning person, like I've said, so I was in and out of the bathroom—I don't know—a bunch of times before she's like, Is everything okay?

Yes, what?

You're going to the bathroom a lot this morning. Can I get in there?

Women, right?

And we're on the sidewalk down on Riverside. The concrete there was perilous; it's coming up at me like a fist; we're on the street with the air settling on our faces like a Wet-Nap.

Hey, I was saying, isn't my buddy Bryan in town?

I don't know, is he?

We're on the train going south, one stop after another, piece by piece a journey into the civilized world, like buttoning a shirt from the top down.

We left the dog asleep at home.

I was thinking, Where did I say we're meeting Bryan again?

You talked to him, Marty, not me.

Did I say that out loud?

Bryan was a guy I'd known for twenty years from publishing. We were fact-checkers together, like in *Bright Lights, Big City*. In the day when people waited a month for a few thousand meticulously chosen words.

So there he was now.

Bryan! Whassup?!

That look on his face like, Huh?

So here's the thing. What I've got in my pants pocket is one of those half-pints of vodka. Which I got I don't know where.

The feeling of having a supply so close to hand was as reassuring as a freaking kitten on my lap. Better, right?

He's a skinny guy, Bryan, paper thin, with a Harvard head on his shoulders and gentle, piercing eyes.

What his people call, I think, a mensch. Gloria loved him.

Gloria was walking with him, in fact. They were in front, then behind me, in impressive good spirits. They talked about Appalachian singers, laughing; what they were doing was pissing me the fuck off now.

I need to find a men's room? I said.

What?

A men's room?

A what?

Here was what I was doing: pissing against a tree on a hill doing that over-the-shoulder, hurry-up bladder contraction thing, and this family walked right past me.

Three small kids, up front this little towheaded muffin with a bow, staring at the steam cloud rising off my antiseptic waterfall of piss.

And her dad picked her up and turned her head away from me. These moments we remember forever. The dad like not even mad, just in damage control; let's keep the kid safe.

Why the fuck was I here.

Who needed this for the rest of my life.

I went to Yale University, people. I had a master's degree in busyness.

In other news, I reached down for my little ampoule of juice and it was gone.

So, Bryan was saying, lunch?

Imagine standing just outside a crowd of people you know but you can't get too close because you don't want them to notice you, and your feet are towel-wrapped hammers installing shelves in the rear wall of your skull.

That horrible moment when you see how drunk you are and can't get away from yourself.

At lunch.

I can't describe the relief to be in that phase of the social encounter where it was acceptable to have a drink out in the open. They were so talky and cliquish I was feeling like they were ignoring me on purpose.

Come on, Marty, Gloria said.

Awkward.

So I said that out loud, too.

What is it like then? Huh? What is it like?

You know, said Bryan after a while, I think you can tell a lot about a restaurant by how it looks from the outside.

What the fuck, I was thinking on the train, did he mean by that?

You've got a mean streak, Gloria said to me, looking me right in the eyes. It comes out when you're drunk.

Oh, my God, I was thinking. So, like, unfair.

I only had a couple glasses. That's hardly—

She was looking at me. We were on the train. There are a thousand stories like this one. Stupid stories so common they don't even have a decent dog fight. So pointless the storyteller can't even remember how they end.

Quiet on the street, but I just didn't hear the vultures circling over my bloody, twitching marriage. Couldn't see the goonies barking in the corner of my living room.

The pink sofa.

Gloria's crying.

She was saying, You absolutely reek of alcohol.

Tell me something I don't—

You know the scary part, she was saying.

No, Gloria, what's the scary part?

You don't even know what you're like. You're such an incredible guy down in there. Such a star. Basically a really sweet man. And you . . . you're . . . like . . . disappearing . . .

Somebody was sobbing. Somebody close.

I forget how it ended.

According to the preamble read before all Alcoholics Anonymous meetings across the world, "The only requirement for membership is a desire to stop drinking."

The fellowship in the 1930s originally had the word *honest* before *desire* but, after some deliberation, decided to remove it. They knew from personal experience that active alcoholics have no idea how to be honest.

That night on the sofa in tears with my wife, I had more than an honest desire to stop drinking.

I had an honest desire to stop breathing.

So I woke up and opened my eyes, and I said, "God, I will never drink again."

And I meant it, again.

And after work that day I was shaky and hot, and I thought, There's one thing that will help me here, just to take the edge off this physical thing, and ease into the new sober me. I can't rush this, could be physically actually dangerous, and so I popped into the bulletproof liquor store on Broadway in my ghetto, next to the closet that sold single-pack vanilla Dutch cigars, and bought a couple three of those airplane bottles of peach-flavored vodka, barely counted as alcohol, and drank them standing on the street between the bus stop and the doughnut place.

CHAPTER FOUR

Alcohol

THE DRUG ETHYL ALCOHOL, called ethanol, depresses the central nervous system. It is a common solvent and intoxicant and is considered a nonessential nutrient. The enzyme dehydrogenase breaks down the ethanol molecule into acetaldehyde, which is then catabolized into acetic acid by a different enzyme. The final metabolic phase is the conversion of acetate into fats, carbon dioxide, and water.

Ethanol's mechanism of action is not fully understood, but it is known to modify cell membranes by dissolving their lipid layer and increasing fluidity. An increase in the action of the receptor GABA is believed to cause the drug's evident impact on behavior.

The effects of alcohol on speech and behavior increase along with its concentration in the blood and are influenced by blood volume, body size, and hydration. Effects at low concentrations include reduced inhibitions, relaxation, and euphoria. At higher concentrations, the drug causes slurred speech and motor impairment, and at levels of about 0.30 percent, it causes confusion and stupor. Blood alcohol levels above 0.50 percent can lead to respiratory paralysis, coma, and death.

Its impact on the life of a chronic consumer, who pounds down drink after drink over a period of many years, are far from euphoric, or even relaxing, particularly to those unlucky enough to be around him. Among adults the most common effects of chronic consumption are dehydration, ennui, memory loss, and liver impairment. Also, the gradual erosion of self-esteem, confidence, any feeling of well-being or sense of hope that tomorrow can be better than today.

Because it never is.

Over time, chronic brew-suckers and winos lose their looks, the people they thought were their friends, their jobs, families, country club memberships, houses, inheritances, coin collections, unpublished manuscripts, shoe trees, and cellular phones.

Eventually, they end up living in a cardboard appliance box on Santa Monica Boulevard with only a single companion until—in the stunning final act of the tragedy that is their life—Animal Control comes and takes away their loyal Bernese mountain dog.

At which point the alcoholic is dead in every way but legally.

Medical science is still far from identifying all of the environmental and genetic factors that cause the disease of alcoholism. Researchers in the field have yet to discover *any* biological treatment or cure. Psychiatrist Carl Jung once noted that he had "never seen one single [alcoholic] recover except through what are called vital spiritual experiences."

Many addiction specialists today claim the best treatment for alcoholics is one in which the addiction is replaced by another, more socially adaptive response. Often, this replacement takes the form of a spiritual commitment that in important ways can mimic the expansive and hopeful effects of alcohol consumption while avoiding its negative consequences.

This spiritual commitment can take manifold forms.

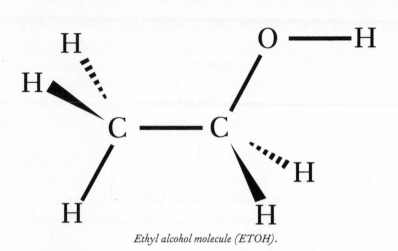

Ethyl alcohol molecule (ETOH).

Bernese mountain dog (HOLA).

CHAPTER FIVE

The Bottom

PEOPLE WONDER WHAT an alcoholic is like and I say: *You.*

We are no different from other people, except we are more afraid.

Alcohol for us isn't just a constant companion, because companions sometimes take a break. It's more like an organ or a tragic past: it's simply always there. A guy named Tony told me that being an alcoholic is like waking up every morning next to a professional wrestler named Demento. It's a life of artificial combat.

Like most alcoholics, I took those quizzes in the back of self-help books and in magazines. Do you black out? Do you sometimes drink by yourself? No sometimes about it, brother. Have friends and family talked to you about your drinking? Have you tried to cut down and not been able to? Are you embarrassed by some of the things you have done while drinking?

Try, like, every fucking day of my life.

Do you try to conceal the amount you drink?

At the end, I dry-heaved in the toilet at work and sometimes spit up blood. I stopped in the Duane Reade on my way home and bought a half liter of generic mouthwash, stepped into a dismantled phone booth on Twenty-sixth Street and Park Avenue South, and swallowed it whole. My head started to shrink. I didn't have a cell phone because I had no one to call. The clawing physical pain in my torso and neck and the nausea that made it harder to focus my eyes—not a symptom, a way of life. Thinking what my boss had said, something like:

Why are you here, Marty?

I . . . because I—

You don't seem to like it. Your work is so-so. You're a smart guy, I know that, but you're just not showing up these days.

Okay, I say. I appreciate that. I'll work on it.

What's going on?

This was a man I admired and liked, and he now knew the feeling everybody close to an active, high-functioning alcoholic knows: *Huh? What am I missing here? What?*

Ask us what's wrong and we'll all say a thousand things: it's the job, the apartment, the husband, the kid, the city, the parking, the consumer price index, the rain. We'll say a thousand things except the one true thing.

Why? Because we can control it; it's not a problem; it's your problem, really, not ours. The entire thrust of most recovery programs is just to slide the addict slowly into the bright light of day, to get him to see his own life and other people as they are. This may not sound like much, but by the end, that life, those relationships—it almost seems better to throw in the napkin.

Why?

Because we do things like this:

I come into the apartment now and step past Hola and Gloria. Don't want her to smell the alcohol on my breath until I've had an official drink, one she's seen.

How was your day? she asks me.

Terrible. I'm in trouble with Don.

What's the problem?

I don't want to talk about it.

I pull out a beer and some cheese I don't want so it doesn't seem like I'm just drinking. I swallow. Now I kiss my wife. That last year I don't know if she had a single sober kiss. We all but stopped making love. Neither of us had the urge, for different reasons; for me, there was always a will but not often a way.

Is everything okay? she asks me.

Yeah. I'm fine. Why?

I leave the beer can on the counter and go into the bathroom. There's a bottle of vodka behind the wastebasket under the sink, which helps. Gloria keeps talking through the door but I don't hear her. I'm sitting on the toilet with my pants up drinking vodka. I flush.

I come out and Hola's standing in the hall there like a little tank with a fluffy tail. Gloria says:

Are you all right? You were in there a long time.

I'm fine.

She's been waiting for you to take her out.

There is nothing I'd enjoy doing less at that moment.

Oh, God, I say. I have a lot of work to do. Can you take her?

She needs time with you, Marty. Why don't you pet her?

I take my workbag into the bedroom and fire up the laptop. I hear Gloria taking the dog out; I hear them come back.

They appear at the bedroom door.

I'm going to listen to some music, Gloria says. You want to come?

Great news. Terrific. I point to the laptop. I've got all this—

Work. Right.

She leaves. Things happen. I take out old stuff I've written that never got published and can't believe my own genius. I pick up the phone. It's my dad. I talk and talk, and he gets very small and quiet on the line. When I'm drunk I talk a lot; that's always what gives me away. If I could just keep my mouth shut, I think, but I can't. I don't remember who hangs up.

Hola lies on the floor staring up at me.

What are you looking at? I ask her.

She stares.

We hit our bottom when we're falling faster than our standards.

Some of us end up in jails or ICUs handcuffed to tables, screaming, and a white light descends. Most of us simply have a moment of clarity or grace, when we see what we are about to lose. Sometimes it's too late.

There's something about Hola's eyes, her sincerity, how pretty she is, lying there on the floor just wanting a daddy. I'm looking at her and I realize I'd talked to my own dad and I don't remember what I said, but he must have known I was drunk. Did he know I was drunk? Maybe I covered it up; it wasn't that much so far, what, five drinks, ten. I have no idea. What time is it? Gloria left did she know I was drunk maybe she didn't know maybe she's not mad at me, and I'm sobbing and sobbing, deep in my heart, just two thousand miles of dirt road and nothing that bad has happened. I'm just tired, and sick, and tired of myself.

I remember Hola jumping on and off the bed. She was hysterical, jumping on, poking at me with her paws, jumping off, running back and forth on the bedroom floor, jumping next to me, poking me, and I was a wreck of a man there with no one and nothing and nowhere to go but back into my workbag for a bottle of—

I don't even remember when I passed out.

When I came to, it was morning and before I opened my eyes I said the first honest prayer I ever said in my life: *God, if Gloria and Hola are still here I will stop drinking.*

I opened my eyes.

CHAPTER SIX

Ballet Dancer

So I don't know who to call or what to do or where to go. I don't know any recovering alcoholics, and I don't want to talk about it anyway, so I saddle up Hola and drive her around the cemetery.

"I'm sorry I've been such a bad dad," I say as we turn up Riverside Drive and the blood-sausage sun punches a hole in the Hoboken skyline.

It's a new day, she seems to say. *A perfect day—just like every other day.*

"I'm . . . I'm going to try to get help. I need help. I'm an idiot."

We all need help, Dad. Think of how much you guys have to do for me. And I'm a very smart girl.

"I feel so bad, Hola. I can't believe I got here. How did this happen to me?"

What's wrong?

"I feel sick. I'm not doing anything right. Gloria's mad at me. I don't have anyone to talk to. My dad probably hates me now. I'm getting old and fat and—"

It's a new day, she seems to say. *A perfect day—just like every other one.*

Letters cannot convey my nausea at work that morning—the throbbing, scraping sickness that claws like a dying Pomeranian in my gut. My usual breakfast is a vanilla milkshake from the McDonald's on Twenty-eighth Street, and I get it so often I don't even have to order. But it doesn't help.

I call my Employee Assistance Plan and tell the woman I want to stop drinking. Only not quite as smoothly as that. She sounds about twelve years old and reads from a script:

"How much do you drink?"

"Is your drinking hurting your performance at work?"

"Have your coworkers talked to you about your drinking?"

A large effort to be honest for once, my voice faltering and barely audible in a vacant conference room with no windows, and what I get from it is nothing at all.

"Okay," says the girl after I've torn secrets from the pages of my soul, "we'd like you to take a brief survey about our customer service today. Would that be all right?"

"Huh? I'm sorry—customer service?"

"Question one," she begins, "on a scale of one to ten—"

"Hold on," I say, "what's the service? What am I supposed to do?"

"I'm sorry?"

"What should I do? For the drinking?"

There is quite a wait and I hear keys tap-tapping as she looks for the answer to this bewildering request. Heroically, she decides to go off script:

"Personally, I'd suggest you find a therapist."

So I do. A large bearded addiction specialist with a lot of credentials and an office across from the St. Vincent's emergency room, now closed, where the creator of *Rent* went to be misdiagnosed.

"So," he says to me, "how can I help you today?"

It seems to me that counselors are overdoing the customer-first thing a bit. I feel like I am walking into Walmart.

I tell him my story honestly and ask him if there is a pill to cure alcoholism. This makes him smile in a way that gives me my answer.

"Addicts always want a quick fix," he says. "That's what makes them addicts, right? But I'm afraid for you it's going to be a slow process. You're going to have to change the way you think."

"What's wrong with the way I think?"

"What you just said."

"Huh?"

"That question," he says. "That's exactly what's wrong."

Depression is anger without the enthusiasm. And I've never been very enthusiastic about therapists. Always seemed to me they were there with the metal toe right at the moment when you're a man facedown on the boards in a room with no light and no heat. Kick. Your worst moment and they want to emphasize, clinically speaking, it's actually worse than you think.

Pow.

Like that psychiatrist I'd seen ten years earlier, the young guy who informed me I was more isolated than your average homeless person.

Ten years ago. He left me with a parting shot:

"One very believable scenario for you," he said, easing my exit paperwork into a thick blue folder, "is that ten years from now, you're pretty much where you are right now."

Only older.

RECOVERING ALCOHOLICS, like children and dogs, require routine.

We talk about getting smart feet—another way of saying if we are to recover, we need to stop listening to our own minds.

Why? Because for many years our best idea was pretty much to have another drink.

I come into my first twelve-step group for the same reason most people do: I can't think of anything else. I don't want to drink more than I don't want to get involved with a cult of the rejected and the damned. My first meeting I come late, sit in the back, leave early, say nothing, and the regulars think: *We'll never see you again.*

Next few weeks I get there on time but say nothing. I don't speak for months, not even to the person on my right or left, much, and the old-timers think: *You'll probably leave. It doesn't work for most of us.*

And when I speak the first time, everybody listens very carefully, and I remember I say: "If I met myself somewhere out there"—gesturing to the world outside the windows, caked with dirt and facing the Juilliard School with its future supernovas—"I wouldn't want to be my friend."

A guy beelines up to me after that and says, "You need to stop saying shit like that. Even to yourself." He is a large man with gray eyebrows and a personality so expansive everyone calls him Crazy Eddie.

What an asshole, I think. What a man who doesn't get it at all.

Two weeks later, a different asshole tells me that I need to hurry up and get a sponsor already because I am making him sad. What I say to that statement is silence.

And the old-timers and the regulars start to think something else now. Something like: *You're right where you need to be—for the amount of work that you've done.*

Before I joined, my image of the fellowship was of a group of old men sitting in a smoke-filled basement complaining about their lives, and I wasn't far wrong. In my home group, I'm considered young: most people insist on taking a lot of punishment before they'll try the rooms. I'm not sure why. We are a remarkably generous, good-natured tribe, in my experience, and as random as a subway car. Darryl is a retired partner in a major law firm; Jeanne was nominated for an acting Obie in the 1980s; Old Dan, when he was Young Dan, was a protégé of William Burroughs and Larry Ferlinghetti; Charlie was Special Forces in Vietnam, then homeless, now a computer systems analyst. Most of us have more ordinary professions, accountants and teachers and social workers. About two-thirds are men, two-thirds over fifty.

Early on, I take a special liking to guy named Clark. He has a rack of suits, for one thing, and refers to books he actually seems to have read. A shortish, brown-skinned man in his late forties, he has tight black curls hanging over a well-worn forehead and a lurking smile. A Mediterranean-looking guy who talks like some boiler room pump-and-dumper, which is not doing him justice; he smells like the richest guy in the world. His shares make me think we have a lot in common: same business school, same disease, same way of relating to the world.

"I may not be much," he tells us, "but I'm all I think about."

Find people who have what you want, they tell us. And Clark definitely has what I want. A successful banker with a good job that doesn't ruin his life, a devoted wife he describes as beautiful but still logical, a young child he claims has no obvious developmental issues, a West Side duplex, and, most impressive of all, a well-behaved boxer named Joey I look forward to meeting someday.

We read the Big Book and *Twelve Steps and Twelve Traditions* and talk about a Higher Power, who we call HP.

"You cannot recover without a Higher Power," Clark tells me. "It doesn't matter what it is. Doesn't matter at all. Only one thing's important."

"What's that?"

"It has to be a power *other* than yourself."

People think of the group itself, the spirit of our cofounders Bill W. and Dr. Bob. It can be a tree outside the meeting room, a voice in the wake of the wind, a verse in red in the book of the Lord—anything, absolutely anything at all.

Except ourselves.

But the real sunlight of the spirit doesn't come from dead people or from inanimate stand-ins for a set of initials we don't understand. The more I experience the fellowship, especially in those first few months, the more I know the overwhelming power of the person in front of us.

Mondays we have a speaker qualify for us, meaning they deliver a monologue for twenty or thirty minutes describing their experience, strength, and hope—or, in the shorthand of the program, what it was like, what happened, and what it's like now. A capsule history of a resurrection.

Strangely enough, although the speakers are as accidental as people on any jury in Manhattan's Southern District Court, almost all of them are graceful, riveting, and sympathetic when they qualify. Drunks are good writers. Susan Cheever has called this "the eloquence we all seem to have when we tell our own stories."

Friends in the program often tell me it was one of these qualifications that caused them finally to accept the possibility that the steps beyond the first half of the first one—*Admitted we were powerless over alcohol*—might be worth a look.

First, I am nudged toward acceptance by a single line in

my favorite book by my favorite author, Susan Conant, who wrote a series of eighteen Dog Lover's Mysteries that I read and reread like some people take bubble baths. In *Stud Rites,* Conant's fictional amateur detective, dog writer Holly Winter, points out that the chair of a national dog show "had been trained by experts: Alaskan malamutes and AA."

Putting AA in impressive company.

And then I hear something extraordinary. I've chosen my particular meeting because it convenes in the mornings, always my best time, and because it is in a church basement near Lincoln Center, home of the New York State Theater and, more specifically, the New York City Ballet. Besides Bernese mountain dogs, these early days the only thing I love is ballet. I'm not sure why; but there you have it: a mystery. Going to the ballet by myself, or with Gloria, I am sled-dogged out of my body into a sphere of absolute beauty I get nowhere else.

One Monday, the speaker is a ballet dancer, a woman in her fifties who had been a soloist with the New York City Ballet years earlier. She is still very slender and tall but has cut her hair short and lacks the little-girl-lost conversational style I'd observed in other retired dancers.

"I drank 'cause I was afraid all the time," she says. "And not really just the performances—I didn't have nerves like that. I was afraid of the other dancers' liking me, the ballet master liking me, was he going to cast me, would I get to go on the tour. It was just this fear I wasn't likeable that made me drink and drug."

I'd hear this over and over again in the rooms, this suspicion we are somehow, on a cellular level, repulsive to the human race. Therapists might call it shame, but it's actually worse than that. It's the original sin.

After I hear the ballet dancer's story, I stop fighting. I remember it now. My on switch turns off. I give something up. For the first time in my life, I feel like I have no control over anything. Only a very, very vague sense of trust in something I do not understand.

I go up to Clark and ask him if he will be my sponsor.

Hola becomes part of this vast dry conspiracy. My group meets every morning at seven a.m., and every morning at six a.m. I feel a set of ivory claws hit my shoulder, and she stands there and screams like a police siren until I physically vacate the bed.

"What's wrong, Hola? Are you okay?"

At which point she catapults up on the bed next to Gloria, lies down in my spot, and promptly goes back to sleep.

Dogs are excellent at knowing the hour of the day, even adjusting for daylight savings time, but they're terrible with weekends, holidays, and the concept of lounging around when there's work to be done. Except for themselves, of course.

Tolerance for their own laziness is absolute.

CHAPTER SEVEN

Graveyard of Gratitude

IF YOU WANT TO KNOW WHY you drink, just stop.

Suddenly, your real life appears. The first person I ever talked to at a meeting, a dapper little man with a bow tie and a drawl, said, "You won't feel better for a while. Many times, your life might seem like it's getting worse. It really ain't, but you'll notice things more. Just don't quit before the miracle."

My friend Amanda, a former national triathlon champion who ended up drugging herself into grand-mal seizures and adult diapers, puts it this way: "Welcome to the jungle."

Envy. Failure. Disappointment. When Thoreau said most of us lead lives of quiet desperation, he wasn't playing colonial kazoo. Do I sound ungrateful?

Ingratitude. When you go into rehab or hook up with a twelve-step fellowship, you're generally told to start pounding out a gratitude list. Every day. You're told to do a lot of things every day, one day at a time, but for people like me this damned list was the most annoying.

"Come on," says Clark one morning, after I tell him point-blank I have nothing to be grateful for. "Everyone has something."

"Exception," I whine, pointing at myself—and don't think I don't see my thumb point up at Whatever.

"How about your health?"

"Feel like shit."

"Okay," he says. He's been here before: newcomers to the program are an absolute cramp in the shorts. "Your apartment. You own it, in Manhattan, greatest city in the world."

"I hate it. It's dark."

"You have a job."

"Yeah, telling people how to sell things on the Internet. I'm using my powers for evil."

"Your wife."

"She's great," I admit. "But she seems so unhappy."

"Like how?"

"She isn't working, just sitting in the back room playing her guitar. She's trying to be all positive, but I feel like it's wearing her out. She needs something good to happen."

"Hmm," he says. "She'll probably leave you."

"Can we move along here?"

"Okay, you went to Yale, wrote for some big magazines, got a fucking Emmy nomination. You got an MBA, published a couple books, pull in six figures. Your parents don't have Alzheimer's; your siblings aren't living on your couch. You even like your in-laws, for freak's sake. You found a way to put down the bottle, and you're not even all that ugly yet."

"Thanks."

"So where's the gratitude, Marty? Things could be a lot worse."

I consider his point. It's always seemed to me that believing things could be worse doesn't necessarily plug in the waffle iron.

He has met his match.

We sit in silence as I contemplate how dismal and rubbery my omelet is, and then the corners of his mouth spasm. He's thought of something.

"I've got it," he says, remembering the only thing I'd ever discussed with him in terms of unadulterated, balls flopping, speed-metal joy. "Your dog! Hola! You're grateful for her."

I shake it.

"Hate to disagree," I say. "She's a monster."

As you can see, Hola is not the monster. It takes me many months to get more grateful and many more to turn the lights on in my apartment, never quite losing the feeling that I have not only missed my cruise but am waiting at the wrong pier, in the wrong city, wearing the wrong pair of pants. It's a common state of mind early in recovery. We go to work and come home, and our heads are open for the first time in years, our eyes are clear, and we look at what we're doing, who we're married to, where we live and say: "How did I get here?"

We look in the mirror and see a guy who's out of shape, has alienated his friends, been written off by his family, has hillocks of debt, capillaries burst at the base of his nose, borderline cholesterol levels, no car, a long historical novel manuscript nobody wants to read, and a wife whose arms and legs are covered with tiny canine-incisor-shaped bruises.

If we're good AAs, we wait a year to make any big decisions, but a lot of us hear that old train coming and jump off the tracks. We quit our jobs. We move away. Divorces are unfortunately common.

Around this time, the economy starts wandering, my wife gets a temporary job working nights and weekends in a gourmet cheese store, and my job doing online marketing at a large Manhattan agency gets so technical it actually begins to frighten me. Hola finds Lyme disease during a long weekend in the Catskill Mountains, where we have a second home called the Rock

House. Each night after work is a tango Argentino to disguise the five doxycycline pills she hates. She gets wise to the peanut butter, the turkey burger, the Jell-O.

Familiar story: middle-aged and underwhelmed. Where's the spirit? Where's the joy? Take a number and wait.

I am waiting, all right, although not for the self-pity to pass. It isn't going to pass. This is the new way of life.

Then Hola jumps up onto the fifteen-hundred-dollar chaise lounge she calls her doggie bed and informs me that things are not as bad as I think. They are worse.

CHAPTER EIGHT

Gloria

OUR APARTMENT WAS CREATED in a week after I'd come home one night half in the paper bag and sniped at Gloria: "This place is a dump. I feel like I don't even have a home." Life with Gloria could tend to be a pileup if you let it go too far. Although everything I said when drunk was said badly, it wasn't all untrue.

She heard my passion and rushed around town with a concept in her head that seemed to consist of a single color and a show business notion of Versailles. Unfortunately for me, the color was pink.

Each day I came back to an apartment simultaneously emptying of brown cardboard boxes and filling with pink wallpaper with a rose pattern, pink overstuffed sofas, and a comfy chair-and-a-half that had an absurdly expensive doggie bed pawed all over it, pink chandeliers with roseate cut-glass shapes dangling over a bed with a pink duvet and shams. The floors were a refinished graham-cracker brown.

I felt like I was living in a crust being injected with raspberry Cool Whip.

Gloria bought paintings of chamber musicians and nineteenth-century ballet dancers with their massive limbs and cartoons from some abandoned romance strip from the golden age of comics. And a small round table inlaid with stones painted with little images of black Maseratis and bikini models.

Sure.

They were pink roses. With the stiff-backed metal chairs with rose cushions, the effect was unmistakable.

"You know," I said, "you turned our house into a French bistro."

We started to refer to our apartment as the Bistro. I had an honest desire to start smoking.

It is after eight on a Friday, one of those warm, damp nights in early fall when Manhattan smells like an open-air restaurant next to a Brazilian yacht club. I've been sober some months now, have entire minutes when I feel almost sane. So I am impressing myself with my own savoir faire as I open the door to the Bistro after a long day of Internet marketing and find myself in a nightmare so dark, so worst-case scenario, even I couldn't have imagined it.

There's a scream from the living room—a woman's shrill scream—and the terrible sound of a wild dog barking, deep and full-throated. I throw open the door and see a tableau:

Hola standing on her rear legs, almost vertical like a human being, her massive forepaws hurtling toward the ceiling, mouth agape and snarling with a wisp of saliva jetting upward, eyes blood pressure red and narrowed into desperate slits, her teeth snapping down like chalk falling on a slate.

Gloria is leaning back, twisting around, her fingers hardened into claws, stepping back into the wall at the moment Hola's teeth crash shut, catching only a piece of her T-shirt and fragments of skin on her upper left arm.

"*Ahhhh!*" she screams. "*Fuck you!*"

Hola drops to the floor and stands there in a four-legged linebacker stance, snarling at Gloria, who is visibly trembling.

"*Hola!*" I shout from the doorway. "*Off!*"

The dog is in that state dogs get into when they're just not thinking. Gloria's eyes are vivid with panic and she turns herself around, facing the wall, her back to the dog, right hand wrapped around her body holding the broken, bleeding skin.

I recognize Hola's body language: tail low and flat, ears back, eyes narrowed and direct, the fur on the back of her neck standing up: attack mode.

I step inside and slam the door behind me. The leash is on the floor just behind Hola—she's backed Gloria up against the wall, and Gloria's not moving—and the noise of the door distracts her a moment. I'm not afraid she'll attack me; she never does. It's always Gloria.

"*Hola!*" I bark out, trying to get her attention off my wife. "*Hola—over here!*"

Easily confused, she turns her head toward me, and I clap my hands and go, "*Ha! Over here! Hola! Ha!*"

I'm just making noise, hoping Gloria can get a moment to run into the kitchen, but she just stands there holding her injured upper arm, cowering against the wall.

I get behind the dog and snatch up the leash. Feeling in my jacket pocket, I'm praying there's some kind of treat, and for once my prayers are answered: part of a granola cinnamon bar. It's out and I'm stepping backward, leaning backward, saying, "Hola, come!"

As soon as the snack appears, she forgets what she's about and raises her body, lowers her hackles, widens her eyes, and trots toward me.

"Sit," I say, and she snatches the treat from my hand.

I lean forward again and, after a few moments of wrestling and wriggling, get the leash around her body, and the horror movie scene winds down.

I look over at Gloria. She's still facing the wall, holding her arm.

"I'm so sorry, hon," I say. "What happened?"

Hola's standing there calmly, staring at my coat pocket.

Gloria's shaking her head from side to side, stunned, as though she just can't talk. Then she turns around and steps away from the wall, and I see her eyes are moist and determined.

"Get her out of here," she chokes out.

"What, hon?"

"I want that . . . *dog* . . . out of here. Now."

"But—"

"Now. Please."

There is nothing for me to do but take the dog outside. I was going to suggest locking her in the bathroom a while, but Gloria seems adamant.

"I'll be right back," I say, having no idea what I'm going to do with Hola.

She pads out happily enough beside me, and I close the door behind us and listen at it for a minute or two—and sure enough, Gloria is crying quietly, gasping for air between almost-silent convulsions. I feel like Hola is gnawing on my exposed, tired brain.

We get outside and the night is offensively beautiful: cool breeze along the Hudson River, lights a-twinkle in New Jersey, the cemetery stuffed with the glorious Revolutionary War dead. I half want to join them.

"This is terrible," I say to Hola.

What, Dad?

"You can't do that. It's not fair."

What did I do?

"You were horrible. You attacked Gloria."

It sure is dark out here. Is that a snowman? I hate snowmen!

What I do is lock Hola in the backseat of the car and leave the window open a crack. "I'll come back for you in a little while," I tell her. "I have to talk to Mommy now. Wait here."

Where are you going? Stop!

When I get back, Gloria is sitting at the round kitchen table with raw eyes but is no longer crying. She's frighteningly calm. Doesn't ask me where I put the dog; doesn't care. Quietly—frightened myself, to tell the truth—I sit across from her, and she looks up at me with a lucid determination, like a lawyer who's sure of the precedents.

Her hands are balled up, her breathing short and shallow.

"How's your asthma?" I say when I can't stand the silence anymore.

"I'm afraid of my own dog," she says. "I didn't want to admit it before, but there it is. It's like it doesn't matter what I do. I'm at the end of my—"

Hold that thought. Tears are back.

So I slide my chair next to hers and put my arm around her, but she shrugs it off, and I'm thinking, *Please don't leave me. Not now. Not when it's starting to change.*

If you want something you never had, you have to do something you never did.

"We'll go back to training," I say, getting an idea. "I'll go this time too. I'll work on the homework they give us. I know I said it was stupid before but—"

"It doesn't work. It never works."

"I'll . . . I'll hire someone to walk the dog for you. You don't have to do anything. I'll take her out early and we'll have some-body come in the afternoon."

She is shaking her head.

"No," she says. "I should be able to walk my own dog. There's something wrong here."

"What about the monks?" I say, referring to the Monks of New Skete, legendary dog trainers and authors who also take in rehab patients. "Or that guy on TV? The Dog Whisperer? We can send her to some camp somewhere. We'll get her repro-grammed."

She stands up, pushing the stiff-backed steel chair away from the table, and glares down with that furious determination I've always admired—except when it's pointed at me.

"It's not just the dog, Marty. It's everything. It's you."

"Me?"

"You're so fucking self-centered. You think you're suffer-ing . . . you're in pain . . . and now you stopped drinking. Well, good for you. But you're not even looking at me. Or Hola. You can't even see us."

"I'm not . . . I don't—"

"What do you think it's been like for me, huh? All these years with you *not even being here?* You weren't a loud drunk—I'll give you that—but you've been ignoring me for too long. And it hurts. And now—now the dog is so horrible. I got the dog—"

She's crying again but doesn't stop talking:

"—I got her," she's saying, "because you were never home. She was going to. Be. My. Friend."

All I can do is watch as she shudders and wipes her eyes with the back of her hand and tries to catch her breath again and again. I want to hug her, but she hates me so much.

Then she says, simply:

"I can't do this anymore. I love you, I think. But it's just—it's too much for me."

And there it is. The words from your nightmare, available now in real life.

I'm starting to stand, say something, when she pushes past me and goes to the door and goes out, closing it behind her, and I hear her walking down the hallway outside our apartment by the time I can move my legs to follow her.

We go together to the car, which is parked on the side of Riverside overlooking the Hudson. A couple times I try to say something, anything, and she tells me to stop. It's hopeless; it really is. I can't remember when I've been so scared in my life. It's like I'm standing in the middle of the Henry Hudson Highway with my eyes closed.

Too late I remember Hola is in the car. Gloria sees her outline in the backseat.

"You have the leash?" she asks me.

"It's still on her."

"Get that dog out of there."

"Listen," I say, suddenly hoarse. "I'll take . . . I'll take her to the pound. Tomorrow. She's not worth all this."

Gloria shakes her head. I'm not sure what she means.

I unlock the car, open the back door, and Hola hops out. Her tail is wagging and her eyes are bright. She's wearing what I think of as her seriocomic expression. It is different from her other expression, with the upturned corners of her mouth, which is simply comic.

"Bye," Gloria says, and she gets into the car.

Hola and I stand on the curb, and we watch her drive away toward the George Washington Bridge.

. . .

Later, after I've fed the dog for the second last time, I look through Gloria's closets and drawers, in a mounting panic, and realize she must have packed all her stuff into the trunk of the Echo before I even got home that night.

CHAPTER NINE

The God Shot

THE NEXT DAY IS A SATURDAY.

Hola gets me up early, although I haven't slept, and I pack her into a rented silver Honda Zipcar whose inside smells like a barn and looks like a lint trap. We pull out onto Riverside Drive and pilot due south toward the North Shore Animal League, because they say they will do everything they can to find the dog a home without having to kill it. I'm not hopeful. They probably won't accept a dog with Hola's temperament. If they don't, I will have to take her to the regular shelter, where she will most likely be put to sleep.

Between you, me, and the sunroof, I have no idea what I am going to do after I drop Hola off, and I'm not sure I care. This is a terrible, empty, airless morning, and it's never going to end.

In the rearview mirror, Hola's grin looks troubled. She's always loved a road trip but knows something is wrong.

"I screwed up again," I say to her. "I can't figure this out."

Can you crack a window back here? she seems to say. *Thanks!*

"Gloria's so mad at me. And you know what's the sad thing? I agree with her. I put her through a lot of—hey, don't look at me like that. You didn't help. It's like we were attacking her from both sides and . . . and . . ."

Don't cry, Dad, says the little Hola in the mirror. *You can't see the road.*

I pull over and wedge the Honda into a slot at the side of Riverside Drive, and with the engine running I let it go like never before: deep, guttural moans that seem to want to turn me inside out. Hola whines too, echoing my feelings. After a while of this, we're cried out. I'm hugging my dog between the seats, and she's got her paws draped over my arms in solidarity.

We're not totally alone, Dad, she's saying. *We have each other. Right?*

"No."

We're totally amazing! I'm just incredible, and you are the best human ever!

"Well . . ."

We just need to prove to Mommy how great we are.

"I don't know, Hola. I can't keep you. It's too late."

You are so wrong, Dad! she says. *As usual. Can we go to the park? Do you have any pretzels? I love you!*

There is a well-established law in the unwritten annals of canine-human psychology that it is impossible to maintain a conviction of universal despair for a significant length of time when you are in proximity to a Bernese mountain dog. Looking at Hola's sincere, tender face gazing at me and then, even more tenderly, ogling a handsome rottweiler being walked past our window, I was able to wipe my eyes with a Wendy's napkin left behind by the ZipCar's previous pilot, breathe in deeply, and feel almost ready to scheme.

What this scheme will look like, I have no clue. Beyond the obvious: it should not involve me drinking again.

"What I see in you," I say to Hola as I pull onto the drive, "I'll never understand."

What do I see in her? It's complicated. One thing about Hola is she is very good looking. This is an objective fact I report. Don't believe me?

So there.

She has big brown eyes that whisper: *You are beautiful too. We can be beautiful together. Do you have any cheesecake?*

Her coat is lustrous and the kind of black that is so dark and pure it looks almost blue. I dyed my hair that color once, when I was sixteen, and I'll never forget coming out of the bathroom and running into my mother. She took one look at the new me and said, "I guess we don't have to worry about you going to the prom this year."

The white blaze on Hola's forehead is narrower than most people like, but it gives her a determined look. And she has what's called a gay tail—meaning kinked—which she proudly holds aloft at full mast, wagging sinuously like a white-tipped flag of triumph.

Dogs have feelings, the same ones we do. It's obvious. They're just much more committed to them.

Hola has a big smile she throws around town like a stack of religious pamphlets. The corners of her mouth elevate, and her head slopes down in that pose horses have when they're super-relaxed. Especially when she is sitting on the bed between my wife and me and we are *both* petting her. That is when the world makes sense.

That moment, she is looking out the window at the deep blue wintery Hudson River and the suspiciously Floridian condos on the Jersey shore beyond.

"Where is Dog when I need Her?" I ask Hola.

Turns out, She is just waiting for the obedience trials to start.

When it was introduced by the American Kennel Club two decades ago, the Canine Good Citizen program was ridiculed by some in the hard-core obedience community.

Many committed trainers saw it as a distinctly second-rate, watered-down, reality TV version of the serious obedience trials that already existed, competitions where precision-heeling dyads earned titles such as Companion Dog and Utility Dog Excellent, and one superdog annually was awarded the title of National Obedience Champion at an invitation-only event. Technically, the NOC isn't limited to golden retrievers and border collies, but it might as well be. A Bernese mountain dog has never even made the semifinals.

And of course, in thinking of the CGC as Obedience for Dummies, these trainers were right.

But serious dog trainers live in an alternate universe where people know what to do around dogs. They know the tenets of operant conditioning and how to get a reliable recall. They know what a clicker is for.

"The competition obedience people thought of the CGC as fine for 'pet people,' " says Susan Conant. "When it first came out, some of them thought that the program diverted owners from real obedience."

Conant's fictional detective says in a book written shortly after the test appeared: "My column [on the CGC] argued that clubs should support the program. My heart, however, quoted Winifred Gibson Strickland, author of *Expert Obedience Training for Dogs,* who says that if something is worth doing, it's worth doing right. Obedience competition is an aristocratic meritocracy, and dogs deserve the chance to earn their titles."

Doubters were missing the point, though. CGC is not about the dog—it's about the human.

This human is a rudderless man-child on Riverside Drive, so I do what we're supposed to do in the program when we don't know what to do: ask for help.

I call my sponsor, Clark, a guy I found myself talking to almost every day, mostly about our dogs.

"I don't know what to do about Hola," I say. "Gloria drove away last night. I think she's scared of the dog."

"Where are you right now?"

"Driving around."

"Your wife left you, and you're driving around? Alone? What don't I like about this image?"

"I'm not alone," I say. "I have Hola."

"Perfect. She left you with the crazy dog. She's a genius."

"She didn't leave us. She's just taking a break."

"They all say—" He stops himself.

I can hear all his possible responses bouncing off the satellite and coming back to Earth. He settles on: "Okay. We can talk about it later. Where are you going?"

"I don't know," I say. "I have to do something about Hola. It's a bad situation. Gloria's scared."

"Everybody's scared of your dog, Marty. She's totally out of control."

"I think she's okay."

"That's 'cause you're a drunk. You're not feeling it. Trust me, someday you will."

Wince. "What should I do?"

"How about some training? Basic obedience work."

"We've done that."

"I've met your dog, bro. You haven't done anything with her."

Thwack. "Whatever."

"Someone's looking out for you, though. Do you know what today is?"

"What?"

As Clark informs me, it happens to be the American Kennel Club's designated Responsible Dog Ownership Day.

This is the kind of coincidence so outrageous that program people call it a God Shot.

The flagship event is being held ten blocks south of AKC headquarters in a beautifully landscaped patch of Manhattan on Twenty-third Street and Fifth Avenue called Madison Square Park, formerly a crack-and-hustler bazaar too dangerous to enter after dark, even with a dog. Clark tells me he'll meet me down there if I want.

We newcomers are told over and over that we need to say yes to any invitation that does not involve alcohol. An alcoholic alone is in bad company, and the AKC officially discourages serving spirits to dogs.

I say, "Yes."

CHAPTER TEN

The Weakest Link

IT IS A CLEAN AND CLEAR DAY, warm enough that the AKC reps can trot around in their bright red T-shirts and blue jeans and not much else.

There are balloons at the entrance to the park and a couple of rings set up with plastic gates, surrounded by a row of black folding chairs three deep. One ring is a demo space for agility shows and fun matches like an egg-and-spoon race for dogs that I assume must be about making scrambled eggs. It has a healthy crowd and an emcee with a working microphone.

The other ring, pushed up against an open-air meat restaurant called the Shake Shack, is some kind of obedience assessment area. The dogs inside this ring are small, and so is the audience. Maybe a dozen people sit or stand around the enclosure, most with dogs, watching with an air of wary expectation.

Reeling Hola on a short leash, I go over to the folding table set up at the entrance to the ring.

A perky terrier-like young woman with no makeup extends an application sheet and pen and says: "Welcome to Canine Good Citizen. Want to take the test?"

"We're not ready."

"How do you know? You could give it a—"

Hola stands up with her paws on the table, snatches the woman's *Daily News* and starts chewing on the *Parade* magazine. It happens, I notice, to have a cover article on Responsible Dog Ownership Day.

"No, Hola!" I say. "Drop it."

She starts enjoying the Sports section.

"Drop," says the woman, in a firm but not very loud voice.

Hola drops the newspaper.

"Back off."

My dog puts four on the floor and stands there, looking up at her new master.

"Good," she says, turning to me. "I see what you mean. You certainly have a wonderful opportunity to train your dog. Do her a favor and teach her some Good Citizenship. How old is she? Two?"

"Um, she's five."

The terrier is stunned into silence.

For the past two decades, since so-called corrective methods have fallen out of style, dog trainers have collectively decided to frame everything in a positive way. So when they tell you that you have a "wonderful opportunity to train your dog," what they mean is that something is very, very wrong.

The woman hands me a pamphlet, and I force-march Hola to the spectator's area and look around the CGC test ring. There are ten cards mounted on the plastic fence at equal intervals around the perimeter, each containing a numbered step. The serious-looking assessors take each dog through the test, make a notation, then pass it on to the next step. A line of five or six dog-owner pairs wait on deck by the check-in table.

The ring itself is not much larger than my apartment, and most of the dogs are those typical Manhattan animal accessories you can carry in a Whole Foods bag. As these yip-meisters go through their tiny paces, I look at the pamphlet, which turns out to be a description of the CGC.

Canine Good Citizen consists of ten tests that seem simple, unless you're unfortunate enough to have an actual dog. In that context, the real test becomes how to ward off clinical depression as you read down the list of requirements.

As I scan it, my mood swings up and down like a chimp at Monkey Jungle, and I begin to get the feeling my father must have had surveying me at my high school graduation—dyed black hair, skinny tie, mounds of poetry, special needs in precalculus—and realizing his eldest son would not only not be going to medical school but might not actually be moving out of the basement anytime soon.

"Don't worry," says a familiar Long Island voice coming up behind me, "it's a lot harder than it looks."

Clark hugs me—men tend to do that in the program—and says, "Right, Hola?"

Hola looks up at him, then back at the ring. For some reason, she hasn't warmed up to Clark.

In the ring, a poodle sits placidly to be brushed and have her front paws examined, one by one. A sheltie mix stands still as her owner shakes hands with the assessor and moves on. A mini-pinscher doesn't jump up as somebody bends down to pet her. A Scottie-Yorkie mix with a button tail lies quietly on the grass as the assessor drops her clipboard behind her (to test "Reaction to distraction"). A nervous-looking Labradoodle nonetheless refrains from whining while her owner goes out of sight for a while (to test "Supervised separation").

"How do they do that?" I ask Clark. "How many do they have to pass?"

"Every one."

I check for sarcasm. "What?"

"It's a pass-fail test. Dog has to pass every one. Ten out of ten. Perfect score."

Darkness falls. Hola can't do any of them. She'd fail before I filled out the form.

Clark says, "Hey, you and Hola should train for this."

"You're high."

"You never thought you'd stop drinking either, right? This has got to be easier."

"Maybe not."

"She's a smart girl. I feel like she has a lot of potential."

There are few people in the world that I trust more than Clark, but at that moment I am entirely sure he is wrong.

What I don't know is that all my fears are misplaced, and I am the one who is wrong. Hola can do all these things and much, much more. Everything she needs, she has, and there is nothing standing between her and a triumphant, a well-ordered life.

Nothing but me.

IN ADDITION to the dog-products sellers and subtalented woofy arts-and-crafts types you find at dog shows, a few breed and other organizations have set up tables. There are reps for Clumber spaniels and the Metropolitan Dog Club—and, unusually, the Bernese mountain dog.

The Bernese booth consists of a sloping card table, a pile of poorly printed color pamphlets, two women, and two dogs. The dogs are lovely, small-boned bitches with glowing coats and tender smiles. The women are at the far edge of middle age with faded short curly hair, Walmart flower-print blouses, sensible jeans, and the no-nonsense faces often owned by people whose dogs respect them.

One of these women turns out to be a legend in the Bernese world, a breeder of multiple champions whose dogs dominated breed specialties in the 1990s. Her name is Lilian Ostermiller of De-Li's kennel, and the previous month she'd been named the AKC's Breeder of the Year in the Working Group.

As I bring Hola up to the little corral where the bitches are sunning, she sticks her nose between the slats and kisses her cousins. She wears her ecstatic expression, and her head is bobbing up and down like I just asked whether she has dance fever.

"They always recognize another Berner," says Lilian. Her voice is clipped and clear and faintly German. "I have a male that barks at any other breed but lets the Berners go without a nod."

"I feel the same way."

"She's being very good," Lilian says, watching my baby. "What a sweetie."

"Oh, she's horrible," I say. "We've tried everything and she doesn't get better. I don't know what to do. She was always like this. In her litter all the siblings were just sitting there, and Hola was running around like a nut."

"Who picked her out?" she asks.

"The breeder."

She nods.

"You know," she says kindly, "we can always see a sucker."

"That's me," I say. "A sucker."

While I stand there chewing on my own regret, the great breeder is eyeing Hola's engagement with her dogs.

"You know," she says, "I like this dog. The ones that just sit there like couch potatoes are too boring. This one has a lot of personality; she's interested in the world. This to me is a great type of dog."

Of course I am shocked to hear my own mini-monster praised by so esteemed a breeder. But not nearly as shocked as I am by what comes next:

"Her problem," says Lilian, "is intelligence. That's a very smart dog you've got there."

I actually look down to make sure I've got the right dog on my leash.

Hola, Clark, and I head for the fenced dog park known as Jemmy's Run, and I let her off leash for some good times. Clark and I lean against the metal fence talking, and I monitor Hola carefully and continuously for signs of funny business.

"I agree," Clark says.

"What?"

"What you're thinking—it's a good idea. The best one you've had this month."

"What?"

"That you should train Hola for her Canine Good Citizen—"

"That was your idea."

"Oh, right. I knew it was a winner."

Now we're watching Hola locked in a full-body clinch with a Yorkie, rolling around and around on the rocky ground like a two-headed furry tornado. "She can't do it," I say. "It's impossible."

"She can totally do it. It's you I'm worried about."

"I'm not the weak link here."

"Yes, you are. You're bad for each other."

I don't have time to respond to this slander before plunging into the storm to haul Hola away from the Yorkie, who emerges from the dust cloud looking like he's won some kind of commendation from the mayor. Hola collapses at my feet, heaving in air, and Clark says:

"Here's the thing. My advice to you. You get this CGC for Gloria. To prove something to her."

"What? That I'm crazy?"

"No," he says, putting his hand on my shoulder. "That you're sane."

CHAPTER ELEVEN

The Test

IN A LETTER introducing the Canine Good Citizen test to dog clubs in 1989, the AKC's then VP of Obedience, James Dearinger, explained: "This program was designed as a response to the anti-canine sentiment that has painfully been gaining momentum these past few years."

CGC was the first AKC-sponsored certification program to open its paws to non-purebred dogs—what the AKC calls mixed breeds rather than mutts. The test, Dearinger explained, focuses entirely on good dog manners and responsible pet ownership.

An early video promoting the test described its goal succinctly: "A dog that makes its owner happy and doesn't make anyone else unhappy."

A test to encourage pet training, as opposed to competitive obedience, was discussed within the AKC as early as the 1970s, and outside the AKC, members of the American Temperament Test Society were advocating a pass/fail test for puppy temperament. Breeders feared that cities would pass laws restricting ownership because of a few highly publicized incidents. The late Herm David, a columnist for *Dog World* magazine, wrote articles about the challenge of dogs living in urban environments and outlined a "good citizen" program in the early 1980s.

The original elements of what became the AKC's CGC

test were developed by a committee that included James Dearinger, Bob Self of *Front & Finish* magazine, and AKC Field Rep Wally Kodis. A pilot was run in 1989 with the Upper Suncoast Dog Training Club in Clearwater, Florida, and early tests were conducted with the Tallahassee Police Department K-9 Unit, a purebred rottweiler club, and the mixed-breed Ochlockonee River Kennel Club. The K-9 dogs passed easily, the well-trained rottweilers all passed, and one-third of the mixed-breed club failed.

As a result of the pilots, some changes were made to the program.

The first three elements were rearranged to a more natural sequence of accepting a stranger, sitting for petting, and sitting still for an exam instead of the original, inverted order.

Strangely, the original test did not include a recall, or come exercise. The reason, says AKC Field Rep Mary Burch, who runs the CGC program today, was that it was considered too basic.

However, she told me, "The club received hundreds of requests from instructors to add a recall, mainly because you really can't begin to train a dog until he comes to you to have a collar put on for training."

Originally, the test included an eccentric item called "Praise and interaction," in which the owner was supposed to play with her dog and then suddenly get it under control, praising its calmness. However, according to Burch, "The more we looked at it, we realized we set the stage for owners to think they should only praise the dog in that test item." There was also the more tactical problem that some breeds, like Labs, couldn't calm down, while others, like basset hounds, "just stared at the evaluators like they were morons."

The most troublesome item, the one that caused most of the Ochlockonee mixed-breeds to fail, was the final one, then called "Dog left alone." The dog was tied to a post for five minutes while the owner waited out of sight. To pass, the dog was not allowed to whine, bark, growl, or otherwise display excessive signs of anxiety or agitation.

This is a difficult item to train and for many dogs to pass.

Susan Conant, who took the test in the early days with one of her malamutes, told me: "Dog left alone was horrible! My Kobuk flunked it. He was tied at the end of a long corridor. He entertained himself by giving a loud concert of northern breed vocalizations. The evaluator let the howling and yipping and woofing go on for the full five minutes." (Kobuk later passed.)

Single-handedly responsible for a majority of the early failures, this item was shortened to three minutes, changed from a tie-out to leaving the dog with "a friendly stranger," and renamed, less fearsomely, supervised separation.

Once the test items were finalized, there remained the significant challenge of socializing it. To this day, external perceptions of the exam—which isn't an obedience title, exactly, and has few obvious, nonspiritual benefits—vary widely. According to an editorial in the *AKC Gazette*, it was originally believed by many that the CGC was a temperament test, similar to the American Temperament Test Society's instrument, and therefore did not require training.

"This view completely misses the point of the program," ranted the *Gazette*. "Dogs are not born trained nor are their owners born knowing how to train them."

Amen.

The test includes a number of basic commands, including sit, down, stay, and come, that no dog knows intuitively. But since there are elements of temperament testing, including accepting strangers and not shying from examination, it is the case that some dogs require less training than others to pass.

As Burch says, "Some dogs don't really have a hard time with the test at all."

And then there is Hola.

CHAPTER TWELVE

Family Manners

FOR A CLASS with such a laid-back name, Family Manners Skills gets complicated very fast.

"This week," says our instructor, Wendy, much too soon, "we're going to practice our lid work in preparation for 'going to mat.' You get the dog to touch the lid with her nose, and click and treat. Then you put the lid on the mat so she targets that, and then you fade the lid. That's when you can start training the down-stay on the mat. It's great for when you have guests, say, and you want your dog out of the way; you just say, 'Go to your mat!' and she goes. Right, Hola?"

This is a class for *beginners*? She might as well have me teach Hola the ancient art of paper folding. We are in Family Manners because it's a prerequisite for the more advanced Canine Good Citizen preparation program, at the end of which the dogs are tested.

Our goal is to take the test in December and invite Gloria, who will then move back in with us for the best Christmas ever. It is now nearly October. We are doomed.

Wendy is a syrupy-voiced fiftysomething woman with limp hair and elastic-waisted jeans, quite slender, unusual in a dog person, with an actual smile—a smile that vanishes with her sentence as Hola, seeing a friendly puss, darts toward her and tries to play some tonsil hockey.

"Make her sit," Wendy tells me.

"Hola, sit," I say, in my ultramanly training voice, which sounds like a cross between Pee-wee Herman and the Grinch Who Stole Christmas. *"Sit."*

To her credit, a vague look of recognition passes across Hola's deep brown eyes before she kisses our instructor on the nose.

Being an expert, Wendy doesn't flinch; she turns away. Dogs understand the cold shoulder better than people do, and Hola falls back on all fours. Turns out the best way to get a dog to leave you alone is to avoid eye contact, a technique well known to women in bars.

"Okay," says Wendy, still facing away from us, "let's see some walking on a loose lead. Use treats if you have to. I'd rather see you cheating with the treats than walking on a tight lead. The dog should be at your side and not pulling. Let's have the Berner show us how it's done."

"Okay, Hola," I say. "It's showtime. Let's go."

She stays.

"Come on, Hola," I say, squeaking up a register. All twenty-two eyes, canine and human, are upon us. "Come on, heel."

Hola starts panting and whining, making a sound that is like a cross between a tiny whoopee cushion and a woman approaching orgasm. (Or so I've heard.) She seems strangely rooted in place, like she is stunned.

"Does she know how to walk?" Wendy asks. "Do you know what a food lure is?"

It would take a very special person not to be able to figure out what a food lure is, but I don't blame her for asking. We are burning daylight here.

"Try luring her out into the ring, slowly, and—"

Suddenly, Hola bullets out, pulling me across the entire

training area and coming to a heroic stop at the accordion gate, where she stands gazing into the next ring, which holds a Canine Good Citizen preparation program. For two long months—an entire semester in the Port Chester Obedience Training Club's Family Manners program—as Hola finds new and amazing ways to display her love of all objects, people, and dogs, I peek longingly at the well-mannered CGC students as they stroll past distractions and sit gently at their owners' sides as they shake hands with one another.

I feel like I am watching *Lifestyles of the Rich and Famous* in a mobile home.

"I'm not seeing much of a loose lead from you guys," says Wendy, who obviously reads a lot of Oscar Wilde. "Does she know the loose lead?"

"Um, we, I mean—"

"Does she know how to sit?"

Okay, now she is getting personal. That is like asking me if I know the Electric Slide. A dog that doesn't know the sit command is basically a dog that hasn't been trained at all.

"Hola, sit," I say.

She sits. Then rolls onto her back and praises the god of her understanding with her four wiggling paws.

Oh, Dad, she seems to say. *I love this class! Thanks!*

It doesn't help that the other pupils are a regular mutt Mensa. In particular, there is a handsome young boxer named Atticus who is obviously most likely to, and I develop what people in the program call "a resentment" (*n.*, homicidal loathing) against him. It isn't just that he is whip-smart, picking up new commands so easily I suspect he looks ahead in the curriculum.

No, it is his loving upward gaze at his owner, a good-looking woman in her twenties who wears a baggy sweatsuit and doesn't seem all that much more gifted than I am as a dog trainer. Well, okay, everyone is more gifted than me, but she is no Siegfried & Roy.

Our only real enemy in life is ourselves.

It amazes me how personally I am taking this dog training thing. Each week, I am nervous for two days before class and ashamed for two days after. Hola's failure feels like an open expression of my defects of character.

And it doesn't help that Clark tells me to give Gloria time. This requires an act of God since, of course, I know her phone number. I rattle around. Work very hard. Talk to Hola. Go to meetings. Look at things Gloria has left around the apartment, her books on Emily Dickinson, hanging files with clippings of reviews of her shows in the *New York Post* and the *Daily News*, pink cashmere scarves and expensive little polka-dot umbrellas, her upright piano in the back room with thick scores of Bach and Aerosmith. Did she ever play Aerosmith?

One day about two weeks after she left, she calls when she knows I'm in my weekly staffing meeting at work and tells me what I'd already guessed: she's living about two hours away in the Catskill Mountains, in our one-bedroom vacation house, called the Rock House because it sits on a rock.

"Don't call me," she says. "Just wanted you to know I'm okay."

I listen to the message a lot but still can't hear the hidden code.

I START GIVING Hola little pep talks in the Zipcar during our half-hour drive up I-87.

"I'm going to need you to bring your A game here, Schmoe," I say to the little Hola in the rearview mirror, using the adorably shortened version of the adorable nickname I give her—Schmola—when I'm nervous. "I'd like you to leave it all out there in the ring, okay?"

Her narrowed eyes seem to say: *What are you talking about, Dad?*

"It's a competitive group of dogs," I say. "A young group. They're going to be training to win, and we need to suit up and show up."

Are we going to the dog park? Are we going to Florida again? Where are you hiding the Pop-Tarts?

"Listen to me. I need you be on point out there. Stay hungry."

I was born hungry.

And inside the facility, it is an utterly woof-centered universe. I don't see any human restrooms, and despite a wind chill in the low double digits some days, there isn't any heat.

Although Wendy doesn't kick us out of the class, she does ask a lot of hard questions:

"Have you done any training with her before?"

"How old is she again? *Five?!* You mean months?"

"Does she have any kind of a stay behavior?"

"Have you ever used a clicker?"

"Does she have a down behavior?"

Everything is a *behavior* with this woman. A down-stay behavior, a long-down-stay behavior, a down-from-standing-and-then-long-stay behavior, a heel behavior, or in Hola's case, misbehavior. Port Chester is an avowedly "positive method" facility: dogs are trained with food rewards and bad behavior is ignored. Wendy's been a click-and-treat operant conditioner so long she breaks life into discrete, reinforceable units, always aiming at what she calls—over and over again—"maximum likelihood."

"Dogs do what gets the cookie and don't do what doesn't," she says. "And the cookie can be anything they want. If you're in the dog park and you call them and take them home, pretty soon they figure out that coming to you in the park gets them nothing they want. You need to cue and reward things like a hundred times in a lot of different places, and eventually you have maximum likelihood they'll do it again. But there's no guarantee with dogs. It's always a choice."

"In fact," she goes on, "what's one way to guarantee your dog will never learn come?"

"I know," says Atticus's owner.

"Anyone else?" Stay. "Just make sure every time you call them you put on their leash and take them home. That will guarantee you never get a recall. Why?"

"Because bad things happen when they come," I say.

"It's like dating. You need four or five good dates before you'll let a bad one slide."

What surprises me is not this wisdom—which, like most dog training, is simply common sense from one foot off the floor—no, it is that Wendy is dating.

Go down, boy, go down! That's a good boy.

Outside class, my relationship with Hola is changing. I'm not sure what I did before on our walks, but it obviously didn't involve the dog.

Now, I watch her hold the city in her paws, breasting the air in front of her proudly like a naval destroyer, capturing everything as her big browns skitter and her mighty proboscis works its chicken bone recon.

Every once in a while she looks back at me—just a glance, to make sure I am still there. It breaks my heart, that glance; how often has she done it before, and I didn't even notice?

CHAPTER THIRTEEN

The Squirrel

HOLA AND I POWER ON. Her sits and downs are marginally more reliable; she develops somewhat of a recall behavior, sometimes even when I call. Her stay shows some palpable potential. I am thinking we might just hammer this CGC thing in a couple of months—

Then the squirrel shows up.

Wendy promises the final class will be a lot of fun, which fills me with a lot of fear. Fun means distractions, and Hola is bad with distractions. She has the attention span of a—well, of a me. I am trying to meditate in the mornings now because Clark says it helps him deal with the stress of Wall Street, but my brain keeps putzing off on tangents. What was I talking about? Oh, right, it is like that.

"How are we doing today, Atticus?" Wendy asks the entire class.

"He's doing great," says the owner of the animal who is, appropriately enough, the teacher's pet.

"What have we been doing this week?"

"Well," starts the owner, "we worked on our go to mat during a big Thanksgiving party. And then I had Atticus mix the cocktails and serve the desserts and post the pictures on my Facebook page . . ." Or whatever. Those two do nothing for my mood, so I tune them out.

"Great," says Wendy. "How's his retrieve coming along?"

Fill in the blank. Hola's retrieve, on the other hand, consists of her snatching the tennis ball out of my cold, tight fingers and shredding it. Lucky for us, retrieve is not one of the CGC tests.

After Atticus has shown us how to be a prima donna, Wendy pulls out a little stuffed squirrel and squeezes it.

Squeak.

My blood stops. Hola lunges to the end of her leash, and only my superior weight keeps her from turning that squirrel into a terrine.

"Control your dog, please," Wendy says.

"She . . . loves . . . squirrels. . . ." Hola's a muscular dog, bred to pull carts up steep Swiss mountains. Maybe if my hands weren't so slippery from all the buttered roast chicken I'd brought for her treats that day, things would be different.

She breaks away from me, running directly to our instructor, and I stare in horror as she throws on the brakes and sits perfectly in front of Wendy, who is holding the squirrel close to her chest.

Collective exhale.

"Hello there," says Wendy to my pet. "What's your name?"

Hola does a down. She stays. Her eyes never leave the squirrel.

"Somebody's trying every trick she has. I'll bet she'd even go to mat right now if she had a clue what that was." Ouch. Hola tries another gorgeous sit. Wendy says, "Dogs aren't that good at discriminating cues. They recognize they've been given *some* cue, usually, and they try whatever worked in the past. That's why it's hard to get them to go down from a stand. They usually cycle through sit first. Hola, stand."

Hola stands.

"Not bad," says Wendy, her eyes widening. "Now watch how she gets this wrong. Hola, down."

Hola goes down.

Moment of silence. Even Atticus appears amazed.

At the end of class, Wendy goes from pair to pair delivering advice on what to do next. When she gets to Hola and me, her expression is surprisingly soft.

"How do you feel?" she asks me.

"Really good," I lie. "I think we made some great progress."

"Okay. What are your goals?"

"Just—I want to work on her manners."

"Great idea."

It feels strangely like that time I sat down with my junior-year girlfriend, Megan, at Sbarro in Herald Square and we both knew it would be our last family-style meat lover's pizza together. Ever.

Wendy is being pretty conspicuous about not recommending our next class, so I decide I'll jump into the canyon: "I was thinking maybe we could try the Canine Good—"

"Here's the thing," she says, lowering her voice. "I have some advice for you. Is that okay?"

"Hit me."

"Dogs are very sensitive, you know."

"And how."

"What you have there is an especially sensitive girl. She's got a set of radar on her that's unusual."

What?

"She's really tuned in to you."

I start to laugh until I realize this isn't 1980s-style irony. "What?"

"Try not to be so nervous in here, you know? Just be calm and have some fun."

"Come again?"

"What I'm saying," she says, "is you're freaking her out. Look at her today—she knows all the commands. That's not the problem. She's hysterical because you are. Think about it."

Stunned silence. Not from Hola, of course, who chooses to prove Wendy right by whining at her retreating, mom-jeaned caboose. Not only has Wendy nailed me, so to speak, but she's said something profoundly depressing.

It would be much easier to train Hola to jump through a flaming tire than it would be to teach myself to calm down. Anxiety is what keeps me alive. Me not all worried and nervous is me without the *e* or the *m*.

THE RIDE BACK to Manhattan is not our best ever. I am surprised how explosively hurt, bewildered, tricked, betrayed, and other adjectives I feel inside. True to her role as my own personal radar detector, Hola sits on the fitted sheet I use to protect the backseat, staring at my head and whimpering. It doesn't help.

Tuned into you.

Be calm.

Have F-U-N.

It is like all those walks with the meats and the stays were a waste of time, like I'd been treating the disease with bloodletting when what it really needed was a sweet dose of something that was no longer in stock.

Clark once said to me: "Marty, you've got more of a theory than a life."

"What does that mean?"

"Read the Big Book. There's a chapter in there called 'Into Action.' There's no chapter called 'Into Thinking.'"

Sometimes I felt like all he'd read were the chapter titles and the slogans they had up on the walls in the rooms—Let Go and Let God, Easy Does It But Do It, It's Alcohol-ism Not Alcohol-wasm—but, hey, it worked for him.

Hola knows Daddy is mad at her, and she seems to have less fire in her eyes as we mount the stairs to go home. Training has an effect like hard physical exercise on dogs. Mental effort takes a bite out of them, and she is always exhausted after class.

Still, she isn't making eye contact, and her gay tail trails limply on the tiles.

I crack open the phone to dial Gloria, and then I change my mind. I don't want my first call to her to be just me complaining about Hola, of all things. Relationships should be about good news.

I don't call her. Which is just my way of putting the ball in her court. I'm sitting at home reading a dog mystery out loud

Life without Gloria.

to Hola, who is asleep, and I'm listening for the phone to ring. Then I realize I am being ridiculous and immature and turn the phone off. But then I think she might call me but not leave a message and I'd never know it, so I turn the phone back on. I put it on the table by my bed all night so Hola and I can hear it if it makes a sound.

CHAPTER FOURTEEN

Sammy the Dog

TWENTY-FIVE YEARS EARLIER:

You couldn't believe a word my mother said, including *dog* and *cat.*

She was an extraordinarily attractive female, like Hola; quite short, with sharp, symmetrical features and large aqua eyes that didn't rest anywhere for long. Like many beautiful people, she was tormented by the failure of a youthful acting career.

Half measures availed us nothing, says the Big Book. *We stood at the turning point.*

She'd grown up poor in Glasgow, Scotland, and her father was a light-boned, red-albino Irishman with milk-white hair since his twenties and wax-paper skin, a butcher when he did work. Missing most of the forefinger on his left hand. Three guesses. Don't show up to work drunk, especially if you work with a meat cleaver.

Our troubles, we think, are basically of our own making.

"I was draggin' me pa home from the pub," said my mother, "and a big dog attacked me. Just came out of nowhere and started snackin' on me wee body like I was a bit of shortbread."

My sister, Cherie, gasped audibly while my brother and I went back to our Mad Lib.

"Oh, my God," said Cherie. "What happened?"

"Not that your brothers would care," said my mother, surveying us with her usual profound disappointment.

"Adjective," I said to my brother, Peter.

"Yellow-bellied."

"A real adjective."

"I was in the hospital for a month," sniffed my mother. "Maybe six."

My sister looked puzzled. "I thought you said you didn't have hospitals when you were a girl. They were only for the rich people and the rotten British bastards."

"Language," said my mother. She always despised the British, or claimed to, though she was vague on exactly why. "We had hospitals. It's just we didn't have any medical supplies. Or any doctors."

"Because of the British?"

"In part," she said, tapering her voice now to let the string section swell up on the soundtrack. "Also because we were very poor. And poor people—"

"*Are treated like shite!*" we all said as a chorus.

"Adverb," I added.

My brother said, "Painfully."

The dog story changed—sometimes she was just nipped on the leg and limped home; sometimes she had to have a blood transfusion and the Rite of Extreme Unction from Father McManus—but the message was always the same:

Dogs are bad. Like the British.

Which is why I was puzzled when a dog appeared one day, hopping out of my dad's gunmetal blue Citroën SM, bounding up to my sister and literally knocking her off the back of her Big Wheel. He was a white standard poodle, obviously no longer a puppy but too zippy to be all that old. Maybe he was one or two.

"This is Sammy," said my father, who in those days was a rather dashing Dr. Kildare type with brown leathery skin and a thoroughbred or two on the side. The dog's only obvious fault, from our point of view, was that he didn't particularly like small animals. "He's a good boy."

Whether Sammy was good or not it was too soon to tell, but he certainly seemed to have a lust for life. He was happily humping my dad's right leg, and he didn't appear to be fixed.

This was when we'd just moved to Michigan, out of South Africa via Queens, New York, and my dad was in the second of a lifetime of mysterious American jobs, this one at a teaching hospital at Wayne State University in downtown Detroit. He was a medical man, and all I knew was that he did research.

"Wow," said my brother. "What kind of dog is that?"

"A big one," I said. Mr. Encyclopedia.

From the start I had a bad feeling about this Sammy situation. For one thing, he never left the house. My mom distrusted and feared him, of course, but on a more practical level she didn't have a clue what to do with a dog. She seemed to think they were just particularly annoying cats.

That which you fear the most will meet you halfway.

"Shouldn't we walk him outside?" asked my brother, the smartest of the three kids.

"Why?" asked my mother.

" 'Cause that's what Mr. Kelly does with Beth's dog every day. Two times."

"Mr. Kelly is a very ignorant man."

What my mother had done was put newspaper down in a corner of the laundry room and encourage Sammy to use it for his show tunes. Amazingly, he preferred other places, including my dad's big leather chair in the living room. That the chair was also brown led to some unfortunate incidents late at night, when my dad settled in to read Gibbon's *The Decline and Fall of the Roman Empire* after his shift at the lab.

"*Christmas!*" he'd scream. To his credit, although my father swore loudly and often, he never used regular curse words.

I turned to Sammy, who was also awake and who for some reason had decided to sleep up on my bed with me.

"You've got to stop doing that," I whispered. "He's going to take you to the pound."

I'm sorry, he seemed to say. *I don't know what I'm supposed to do.*

"You and me both, boy. You and me both."

MY SISTER TRIED to play with Sammy after school while my brother did his advanced math problems and I surveyed the scene ironically.

"What are you doing?" I asked her.

"I'm teaching him a trick."

"What kind of trick?"

"As a matter of fact, I'm teaching him mime."

"That's ridiculous."

"You only think that 'cause you're retarded."

"You're retarded."

"You don't know anything about dogs."

She was right, of course, but I knew she would totally fail. This was a dog who didn't know a single command—whose *owners* didn't know a single command—and who lived on cuff links and the bowls of Cap'n Crunch I fed him. The only exercise he got was when he dry-humped the floor-model Electrolux.

Peter was the one who noticed the change. It was subtle,

the first time. Something not quite describable but nonetheless there. More on the inside than the outside. One day Sammy was different.

For one thing, he seemed a little smaller. For another, he was scared; twitched every time a car passed. He looked haggard and haunted—like a dog on the run from the law.

"What's wrong with Sammy?" asked Peter. "He's not chewing on my lift tickets. And look—he did it on the newspaper like he's supposed to. He lost his spirit."

Suddenly, my mom got very busy arranging our after-school chocolate cupcakes on a plate. I should have been suspicious: they were the enormous Superman-themed cakes from Machus Bakery.

"Sammy's sick," I said that night at dinner. "He doesn't like Cap'n Crunch."

"Absurd," said my mom. "Everybody likes the Cap'n."

"Not Sammy. Not anymore."

Eventually, we found something he liked—Cheez Doodles—and my sister got him to do a pretty good sit by pushing down on his haunches. The fact that any dog sits when you do that didn't detract from her sense of triumph.

"Look!" she screamed. "Sammy's sitting! Look! You're not looking."

A few days later, the dog had changed again. He still had the haunted, witness-protection look, the hollow eyes, the droopy whiskers that told of bad decisions that had crossed state lines. But there was something else, too.

As usual, my brother noticed it first.

"Hey, what happened to Sammy?" he asked. "He's a different color. He's, like, blue or something."

"That's ridiculous," said my mom.

"What, did he roll around in something?" Peter ran his right hand over Sammy's curly pelt and then examined it. "Nope. No residue. He's clean."

My brother always spoke like he worked for the Justice Department. He wasn't even a citizen.

"Why is he growling?" asked my sister.

"Oh, Jesus, not again. Stop growling!" my mom snapped at me.

"Not Martin, the dog. Sammy's growling."

"It's probably hunger pangs," I said, optimistically searching our cabinets for some King Vitaman.

"Maybe he doesn't like being blue," said my brother.

My mom swung around with a kind of desperate, half-cocked look in her eye that made us focus on our snack cakes. "Could you children please be quiet?! I can't hear myself cook here."

"There's no doubt about it," I said after a moment. "Sammy is a different color."

"He's blue," said my brother.

"You know what I think," said my sister, who tended to say the things others feared to say, usually when her mouth was full. "I think that isn't Sammy."

We were in the living room teaching Sammy backgammon one day when my dad came home and said he had some news for us.

No news was good news in that family. We tended not to make flat-out statements of fact unless the cops were in the driveway.

"I'm afraid I made a mistake," said my dad. "I . . . you see, I . . . I promised Sammy to another family, another little girl, and I have to give him back. But she's very thankful you took such good, uh, care of him. But I have to give him back."

My sister burst into tears, and my brother started to argue.

"That's not Sammy anyway," he said. "Make sure you give her the right dog."

My dad left with the poodle right then and didn't come back till the next day. That wasn't unusual. His shifts at the lab were strange, and we never knew quite where he was.

Be fearless and thorough from the very start. Do not be discouraged.

Did we miss Sammy? Although my sister cried for two days, and I did not, I felt a warm and constant ache for a good long while, especially at night. It's only looking back that I can see what it meant. I didn't know yet just how lonely I was, how much I needed someone around me who did not wish, every night, that the night would go on.

I've never known a dog who didn't say *Good morning, God!* Rather than *Good God, morning.*

But years later I got a hint, a confirmation of what happened to Sammy. I was quizzing my dad on his days in Zambia, where he'd pioneered some transplantation techniques, and I asked him how he practiced.

"There weren't all those silly laws in the bush," he said.

"You mean malpractice laws?"

He winked at me.

"Let's just say the sick people there were grateful for anything. Even if we hadn't quite worked out the kinks. Very disappointing when I got to America."

Bad moment. My dad always said America like it was the name of a virus we'd caught at JFK Airport in the late 1960s.

"How so?"

"We couldn't use human subjects anymore," he said. "So we had to use dogs."

CHAPTER FIFTEEN

The Working Weak

DON'T DRINK; go to meetings. Go to meetings; don't drink. Call your sponsor. Walk the dog; train the dog. Work. Don't waste time thinking about what thinking cannot change. Move a muscle; change a thought. It's into action—not into thinking. It occurs to me more than once that the program works for me in those early months only because it keeps me so freaking busy with annoying activities—go to meetings; call your sponsor; hit ninety meetings in ninety days; write a fearless and searching moral inventory; sleep; work your fourth step—I don't have a spare moment to walk over to the liquor store.

Gloria is ignoring us. I feel like a man at the bottom of a well.

I don't like my apartment anymore. When Gloria was there, I looked forward to going home. She was a big improvement on Internet marketing. Now my walls and I are at odds. I'm training the dog. I'm rereading a Susan Conant mystery. I'm sleeping. Waiting. This is my life.

For some reason, showing up sober improves my performance at work. People comment on how "rested" I look. I'm going softly insane. Which is the only explanation I can give for what I decide to do next. It's entirely whimsical and without point. Maybe that's the point. I don't know.

I decide to single-handedly create a word and use word-of-mouth (what we call WOM) and viral online marketing

(VOM)—which is, after all, my job—to seed it into the culture. Think of it as office-based performance art.

There is a young woman who works for me at the marketing agency, twenty-six and a Harvard Business School graduate—very competent and connected, with lavish auburn hair and JLo-like frame, no makeup, one of those lawyer's kids who seem older than their years because of ugly divorces and being smarter than their friends.

I'm noticing one day she has over one thousand friends on Facebook.

"Wow," I say, "that's a lot of friends."

"Not really."

"How'd you manage that? I don't think I've even *met* a thousand people."

"Well, I've been on since the beginning," she says. "It started as an all-Ivy networking site. I was in college. It was very smart. Marketing went through connecteds and word of mouth and . . ."

She is always raving about somebody or other's WOM and VOM strategy, so I watch her lips move for a while.

". . . just need to figure out a revenue model."

"Totes," I say.

A moment.

"What?"

"Totes. It's like *totally,* only shorter. Everybody's saying it." She nods, dubiously. "Right."

I've noticed if you mention everybody's doing something, and it's a remotely good idea, eventually somebody starts doing it. Thus, I wasn't exactly lying, just playing with the element of time.

And for a few weeks I make an effort to place this word in strategic locations in my speech.

A coworker says: "You know, MySpace is so over."

"Totes."

A client: "Let's regroup next week to talk about how we can work social into this campaign."

"Totes."

At the vending machine in the pantry: "All these little coffee packs are the same. They don't taste any different. It's just marketing."

"Totes."

One night, as nervous as I was on our first date, I call Gloria. She picks up and says: "How's Hola?"

"I'm doing okay."

"And how are you?"

I realize the silence is more what I want than the words; words strap us to their meanings, which are never quite what we mean, since we didn't invent them, just inherited them from people we never met. Except for *totes*.

"I'm working on Hola," I say. "She's doing better."

"That's good."

"Much better."

"Okay."

Crickets. "Do you want to see her?"

"I'm thinking of staying out here a while. Just to . . . figure things out."

I'm thinking: This is not fair. I'm conscious of something fragile connecting us and if I move or even think too hard it's going to break.

"Her training is going well," I say. "The teacher said her recall is better than her own dog's."

"The teacher?"

"We're taking a class."

"Okay."

"Yeah," I say. "How is it up there?"

"Good. It's good." Bop. "Are you still going . . . to those meetings?"

"Yeah. Every morning. It's good."

"How're you feeling?"

"Better. Good. You?"

"Riding a lot."

"Nutmeg?"

"Brenda has me on a new one now, Blackie."

That time she had her mother write me a formal invitation to visit them in Iowa for Christmas, me so shaky from my first rehab, just looking at her mother's perfect penmanship, wheels touching the runway like a hand on my back.

"Who's Blackie?"

"You haven't met him. He's bigger than Nutmeg, but he's a great horse."

Telling me a thousand years ago, in the world's worst apartment on St. Mark's Place, across from the old Kim's Video: "You're crazy about me; stop trying to convince yourself that you're not."

"How's Brenda?"

Something about her kid—Gloria has an antifetish for riding instructors' seven-year-old children ordering her around in their little generals' voices during her lessons, something she claims has become an epidemic. In fact, she thinks that kids have gone wild. Her idea of an ideal parent is the Fran Drescher character in *The Nanny*, which she watched religiously every weeknight at 11:30 p.m. and again at midnight. When she lived with us.

"And how's Samba?" I say. "Tim and Andrea?"

"Good. I'm going every day. I got a part-time job there—"

"*Job?*"

"Just on Sundays, four hours a week. Helping with the empanadas."

"That's part-time all right."

"Like I said."

"Are you . . . ?"

And I'm thirty again, starving myself, she's sick all the time, we have no health insurance, I'm working overnight answering questions about word processing, she's picking up phones at the last public riding stable in Manhattan, now deceased, and there isn't a day I'm not grateful I have her voice to listen to rather than the ones inside my own head.

"What?" she says.

"Nothing."

"I have to go now, Marty."

"Yeah," I say. "Sure."

"Take care of yourself."

"Totes."

CHAPTER SIXTEEN

Dog Camp

THE BIG-BONED OTCH handler scans me up and down and says, "Hey, sit here—a guy!"

So I sit next to her at the round table in the cellar of a hunting lodge in the middle of Virginia, listening to the dog-obsessed, and I'm realizing that to count as a sex symbol in the world of dog training all you really need to be is male. The dog training magazine *Front & Finish* recently ran a survey of its readers and discovered more than 90 percent were women over fifty. Competitive canine obedience is overwhelmingly a sport for postmenopausal women.

Continuing her conversation with the nun, in full habit, the handler says, "I won't do the NOI anymore. It's too hard on the dogs. Seven straight hours of drills over two days. A lot of the OTCH handlers push their dogs; they're nasty and competitive. There was this dog called Zipper you used to see all over the place; he just disappeared. They're pushed and proofed and corrected half to death. Eventually, they just won't do it anymore."

Outside, through a wedge in the top of the cellar window, I see a steep green hill leading up to our lodging for the week: stark hunting rooms so humorously heated Hola and I will not age at all during the night.

And behind them a mountain of forest so fertile it's liquid.

"Uh, really?" I say.

The big-boned, child-faced, retriever-like handler taps my fingers lightly as they come to rest on the tabletop.

"There's no friendships among the OTCH types. It's kind of ugly at the top."

OTCH: Obedience Trial Champion, the highest level a dog can earn in canine obedience trials sponsored by the American Kennel Club. NOI: the annual National Obedience Invitational, to which my new friend is evidently invited. Making her very, very successful indeed in this subculture of serious dog trainers.

She takes her hand off mine, peeks at my name tag, saying, "So, Marty, why are you here?"

Even the nun leans forward in the din to hear this one.

What I'm doing is feeling chopped up.

Hola's in the lodge, sleeping on top of the bed, a narrow double bed that already feels empty to me.

The camp is a six-hour drive due south from Manhattan, and Hola cries the whole way.

She doesn't eat lunch; she doesn't stand on the backseat gazing at the passing pageant of life, as she usually does when my wife is driving.

And I feel nothing but guilty, because her mood, as Wendy told me, is just a theatrical amplification of my own. Even Gloria knew this: she used to call Hola my radar detector.

Somewhere south of Baltimore, I call my sponsor.

"Where are you going?" he asks me.

"Dog camp."

"What now?"

"It's a camp for dog training run by this famous couple. They have their own method, called the Motivational Method. It's supposed to be great."

"You took off work for this?"

"Yup."

"How long?"

"A week."

"I repeat: Why?"

"This couple wrote the only book there is on the Canine Good Citizen. I'm hoping they can help me get Hola in shape."

"Again," says Clark, again, "why?"

"I don't know," I relent. "I need a change of scene. Work makes me crazy. Hola's down-stay is weak."

"Sounds like a fucked-up idea of a vacation. They have any meetings out there?"

"It's in Virginia. The middle of nowhere. I don't want to go to some hillbilly, *Deliverance* meeting."

"Don't be a snob. You can call people, right?"

"Probably not. It's the middle of—"

"This doesn't sound good to me, Marty. We're only an arm's length away from a drink all the time."

"How am I going to get any alcohol? I don't see any stores—"

"Where there's a will," says my sponsor, "there is always a way."

We wend through twisted hills stuffed with impossibly green vegetation. Noticeably damp, pregnant trees and grass, as though the leaves have been lightly steamed. Passing through towns that look like they were built by eccentric billionaires for a boom that never quite arrived. Thrown up in a day—new gas stations, hospitals, schools. Elegant strip malls with leafy wainscoting and full-bodied pines.

But no people.

Then we round a corner past a tumbledown hog farm, and there's the dog camp: a two-story wood-framed hunting lodge with rows of gray-trimmed windows, and behind it on the foot-hills of a steep dark mountain loaded with lumber, two long buildings that resemble the original Bates Motel.

Big dog events tend to be held in places humans abandoned in the 1950s—out-of-the-way, downscale locations with no heat, no cellular reception, no TVs in the room, no Internet, no tiki bar or hot tubs or robes or room service.

But they all have the most unusual amenity of all: they allow dogs.

I pull into the parking lot crammed with ramshackle campers larded with bumper stickers like I Brake for Yorkies and Dog Is My Co-pilot, roll down the window to give Hola some air, and go into the lodge. It has a narrow hall and paeans to Graves Mountain's storied past, which seems to involve a lot of very severe-looking tall men with beards and long guns.

There's no line in front of the card table marked Reception, behind which sits an elderly woman wearing a tan Graves Mountain polo shirt and bright pink lipstick.

Right away there is a problem. A pennant tacked to the wall behind the women reads:

"Welcome Back—Volhard Instructor Training Camp"

See the problem?

"Instructor?!"

"Hello there," says the woman. "What's your name?"

After telling her, I say, "I'm a regular person."

"Good for you."

"I mean, I'm not an instructor. I just want to learn the Canine Good Citizen."

"Don't worry about it," she says, handing me my plastic name tag and a silver bag of canine nutritional supplement. "You're a serious dog trainer. That's all that matters."

"I'm not that serious."

"Ha," she says. "Ha, ha."

Dinner is family style, at long tables, with the deep-fried dishes being passed around relentlessly and scooped onto plates in a way that reminds me of my elementary school cafeteria back in Birmingham, Michigan.

The scene also reminds me of Holly Winter's observation: "My lackadaisical attitude toward my own diet had been in total contrast to the care I devoted to making sure that my animals received optimal nutrition."

There's a Texan mother and daughter across from me at dinner, and it turns out the daughter will be in my class.

"I want to do the CGC," I say.

"We have that," says the daughter, a languid, worried-looking, Polish-Hispanic woman of about thirty. "We have that on both my sheperds. I don't know how. One of my dogs nipped at another dog during the test."

"Oh my God, we almost failed ours," says the woman on my left, a retired schoolteacher named Beth who runs a big dog training center in North Carolina. "My Bobo was doing great until the separation and some kid walks by eating a hot dog. He almost tackles the kid to the ground. It was incredible—"

"Many a perfect two hundred obedience run has been ruined by a hot dog," says a voice from the end of the table. He's a big, wearily handsome young guy wearing a leather cowboy hat he never takes off; all week, people just call him the Cowboy.

We overeat and talk entirely about our dogs, and I'd be lying if I say I feel entirely at home.

We have a common cause, of course, but these people are a lot more knowledgeable than I am. I silently vow to keep my mouth shut and listen, as they advise newcomers to do at twelve-step meetings—a vow I break right away.

Beth is talking about a Bernese mountain dog in one of her classes. She says, "The owner just did not have control of that dog. Their previous one was real mellow, but the next one they got was a total maniac and—"

"Hey!" I bark, spraying remnants of my Jell-O pie. "That's like me. I got one of those. I've been trying for a while now and can't get her to do much. She untrainable."

Awkward silence.

Right away, I realize what I've done: committed the beginning dog trainer's crime of blaming the victim; the problem, they're all thinking, is clearly not with the dog.

"In eight weeks," Beth continues, "that Berner earned her Therapy Dog."

The rest of the week, I try to act more like a lawn than a mower.

I HAD HEARD there are more than one hundred dogs at the camp, and the dining room is wall to wall with trainers. Though I scan the crowd, I can't see our hosts—the great Jack and Wendy Volhard.

The Cowboy says, "I hear Jack was a judge for, like, twenty years."

"AKC?" Beth asks.

"No, humans. A circuit court judge."

"I hope he doesn't judge my dog," says the Texan girl.

"Oh, he will."

"I saw them speak once," says the woman on Beth's left, a meek-seeming personal assistant named Kelly who was too afraid to bring her dogs and so is attending camp as an observer.

"Where?" I say.

"It was a train-the-trainer thing. I lied so I could get in, said I was a dog groomer. They were amazing. I'll never forget it."

That night I take Hola for a walk on the absurdly steep, dew-slicked hill leading up to our cabin.

The large and small dogs have been separated into different compounds, probably because the small-dog owners are embarrassed. Both compounds sit at the foot of a thickly wooded pair of mountains necklaced with hunting paths and rapid shallow streams, dirt paths paved with grassy clumps of horseshit and dead leaves.

We run into a woman walking two gorgeous Swissies, which are related to Bernese mountain dogs and look just like Hola with a close crew cut.

"She's quite a handful, huh?" asks the woman, a tired-looking fortysomething wearing a new Rutger's hoodie and a big diamond wedding band.

"Yeah, she's a pistol."

"How old? Two?"

"Everybody says that," I say. "She's five."

"Amazing."

"We want to get our CGC."

She looks at me cautiously as I struggle to pull Hola away from her dogs. "You taking the test here? They give it at the end."

"I don't think we're ready," I say.

At this point Hola hurls herself through the air, landing on the back of one of the Swissies, who shrugs her off, steps back, and sneers: definitely not on the guest list.

"Yeah," says the woman, "I see what you mean."

CHAPTER SEVENTEEN

The Motivational Method

NEXT MORNING, we walk on the vertical hills under skies so clean they could treat an open wound, our four sleep-dried eyes blinking out at ropes of small farms that probably haven't changed much since the Civil War.

"Hola," I say. "I'm sorry I made you come here. I'll try to make it fun."

Hey, she says, *don't worry about it. I'm always up for a road trip.*

"You seemed upset in the car."

I miss Mommy.

No comment.

Are you by any chance hungry?

"Maybe we'll learning something," I say, not really listening to my dog. "Let's keep our ears open."

Oh, was that the breakfast bell?

And then I'm sitting at the round table in the cellar next to the big-boned OTCH handler, Stella, and the nun, Sister Irene, who runs a thriving kennel in upstate New York, and we're listening to Jack and Wendy Volhard introduce us to our coming great adventure.

Wendy is saying, "Wear waterproof shoes. Most of your

classes will be held outdoors no matter what, and the grass gets very soggy. Keep your dogs dry in the room when they're not working."

She is a lean British woman, serious, calm, and physically stolid, and we listen to her with keen attention, leaning forward. Her cheekbones are sharp, her voice carefully modulated, and immediately I recognize what she is: pure alpha female.

"Watch out for doorways," she says. "Dogs confront each other at thresholds, doorways, exits, jumping in and out of cars."

"There's no TV here," she continues. "No phone, although if you walk around in the parking lot you can sometimes get a signal. News is stress. Live like your dogs for a week."

"That was stirring, my sweet," says Jack, who unfolds his long frame and beams at us. He's a palpably youthful old southern gentleman with a close-cropped silver beard and a buoyant sense of humor, like a yang to Wendy's yin. Wendy sits and gazes up, way up at him. We are obviously eavesdropping on one of the great romances.

"How many of you," Jack asks us, "work your dogs three hours a day?"

Of maybe sixty people in the cellar, only one guy raises his hand—a hard-ass-looking dude wearing fatigues who, I hear later, owns a flower shop.

"At the Volhard Instructor Training Camp," Jack says, "we work the dogs very hard. On day two some of you will show signs of fatigue. You will take it out on the staff. This is normal. We will ask you to refrain from physical combat."

"Day three," he says after the laughter dies, "the dogs will start doing the same. They have a longer fuse than we do."

He explains the classes offered, which with the exception

of the basic level Hola and I are taking—ironically called Fast Track—conform to the three standard AKC obedience classes: Novice, Open, and Utility.

"The difference between Novice and Open," Jack says, "is the addition of jumps to the basic heeling patterns and commands. The difference between Open and Utility is you must have a retrieve. [Beat.] On command. [Laughter.] We require the *re* part of the exercise."

For a dog trainer, this guy is a first-rate comedian.

Jack and Wendy Volhard are the Bill and Hillary Clinton of canine obedience, a long-married couple whose books, videos, and seminars have saved more than twenty thousand of us dog owners from ourselves. Pioneers in puppy temperament testing, canine nutrition, and alternative healing, they are also coauthors of the book that tops my personal canon, after the mysteries of Susan Conant, namely, *The Canine Good Citizen: Every Dog Can Be One.*

I talk to Kelly, the dogless personal assistant, during the break, establishing that even she knows more about dogs than I do, and then Stella storms back and sits with a deepening despair.

"That nun," she says, "is a real piece of work. She grabbed the only land line we can use in this place. She's standing there yelling into it like some . . . some guy at an auction—'*Sell! Buy! Sell! Nail them to the fucking wall!* I don't give a shit what they're offering, it's too fucking low.' "

"Wow," I say. "I'm not sure those words are in the liturgy."

"Jesus never mentioned dogs," says Kelly, and I think: a born-again.

"I'll tell you what," says Stella, "if that nun hogs the phone all week I'm going to nail *her* to the fucking wall."

"Ha," I say, as Sister Irene returns to her seat with a beatific glow.

Then Wendy stands in front of an empty whiteboard and introduces us to the real sacred mysteries:

"Dogs think, reason, and have a language," she says. "It's called body language. People also have this. Within a few seconds you've sized someone up as a type based on their body language."

Yes, I think, seeing how I've already categorized a lot of the people in the room as poor spellers without even talking to them. In fact, talking makes it harder: it's a mess of contradictions.

She says, "We're going to spend the whole week making you untwitch. Most of us are moving all the time without knowing it, and our dogs pick up on everything. We confuse them. Leaning in a quarter inch can make a difference to a dog. Every motion we make must have a clear purpose and meaning if we want to communicate."

She was originally inspired, she tells us, by a course she took in the 1980s with a German policeman named Jorg Silkenath, who practiced a method of training called Schutzhund.

"He didn't talk at all," she says. "It was purely communicating with the dog through motion. He said it was a secret method that was passed down from generation to generation. That you needed to apprentice to a trainer, like the old guild system."

"None of what we teach here is new," she admits. "It's just nobody wrote it all down before."

Another inspiration was the Austrian behaviorist Konrad Lorenz, whose classic *On Aggression* divided animal behaviors into discrete groups he called drives, which are present, to a greater or lesser extent, in each animal.

"All dogs are individuals," says Wendy. "No two are the same. Once you know their personality, defined by their drives, you know what kind of training to do. It will cut training time in half, without stressing the dog. A stressed dog doesn't learn."

Hola is stressed. She's always stressed. Florence had told me the last day of Family Manners that this had something to do with my own personal anxiety, but I wasn't sure what to do with this insight except worry about it.

"There are only three main drives," Wendy explains. "There's the prey drive, which is the instinct that makes them go after balls and shake T-shirts like a dead animal. Then there's pack drive, which is about reproduction, nurturing, their status in the group. And there's defense, which is either fight or flight. It's about self-preservation.

"All these drives are basic to the animal's survival, but every individual is higher or lower on each, and you need to understand where your dog is to train them effectively."

"It's sad," she says, "but over time a lot of the defense fight/flight tends to get bred out. We're left with animals who are not animals. The ASPCA kills off dogs with some oomph. What's left are dogs who are brain dead. You need some oomph to be good at tasks."

I remember something Susan Conant wrote: "You can teach a dog to quit the theatrics, but if he doesn't have any zip to begin with, he never will."

Zip is something my Hola most definitely has.

"We can use our dog's drives to train them," Wendy explains, "by knowing which drive to elicit in the given circumstances.

"When your dog's with you, he must be in pack drive. Your body must be quiet, not moving, absolutely still and straight. So many beginners make the mistake of yelling *Come!* and leaning forward. To the dog, these are opposite signals."

The AKC Novice exercises, which lead to the title Companion Dog, or CD, are mostly pack behaviors, she tells us. "Heeling patterns, figure eight, stand, recall, stay—these are all pack behaviors.

"When you add the retrieve in Open and Utility," she continues, "it's a prey exercise. Now, the lower your dog is on defense, the more body language you need . . ."

It gets a lot more complicated, and at some point I stop taking notes.

A stressed dog doesn't learn.

I feel like I can pass as a legitimate participant in this crowd until we take our dogs out: the moment I'm on the field trying to switch Hola from prey into pack by heeling her in a tight circle to the left—which is what, apparently, works—she is going to betray me.

Totes.

AND SHE DOES.

Turns out the only people more punctual than AA members are dog trainers. At one minute before nine, the entire Fast Track class is assembled in an attentive circle in the enclosed picnic shed at the foot of the hill, beside the babbling brook. There's about twenty of us, mostly women, most with larger breeds, including five German shepherd dogs, two Belgian Malinois, some field Labs, a collie, and an enormous white polar-bear-looking thing I've never seen before and hope never to see again.

The dogs are groomed to within an inch of their lives, but the owners look like they just rolled off a bunk after two weeks at sea. They drive dog-stickered vans with room for extra crates and wear loose-fitting sweatshirts that say cute things like You Had Me at Woof, and their notebooks have laminated pages. They have notebooks.

Meanwhile, I forgot my pen, don't have the right shoes, have a car that's too small for Hola's crate, which I didn't bring anyway because she refuses to get into it.

"Welcome to Fast Track," says our instructor, Mary Jo. She's a springy, bell-shaped, loud woman with an infectious dog joy and a national reputation for teaching stupid pet tricks to small dogs. Rumor is, she trained the first President Bush's famous springer spaniel, Millie.

"We're going to start with the sit," Mary Jo says. "Let's begin by kneeling down next to our dogs, like this. Put your hands gently on their rear legs and guide them into the sit."

I think: *What?!*

Hola knows sit; she knows it in her sleep. But I was always told to stand facing her, raising my palm, say, "Sit!" and then give her a hot dog.

First problem—no hot dogs. Second problem—no standing. Third problem—really, the primary one, if you are observing us, as Mary Jo and her assistants pretty quickly are—is that Hola is *hysterical*. There's no other word for it. She's pulling me left and right on the leash, spinning around, all the while emitting a high-pitched squeal that can probably be heard in Richmond.

"Shit," I say to her. "Stop it!"

As Mary Jo moves onto the down, her assistant, Sally, peels us out of the circle and off to the side.

"You're a leaner," she says to me. "Stop leaning."

"But Mary Jo said to lean over her."

"It's not a lean," she says. "It's a crouch. Body straight. Like that. Okay."

I try to grab Hola's back paws, but she snakes away and explodes to the end of the leash. I stand and reel her back in.

"Imagine how you'd feel if a big man was leaning over your head like that," says Sally.

"Not so good."

"Someone five times as tall as you are."

"I see what you mean."

We try it for an hour or so next to the wall of the picnic shed, to give Hola fewer options for escape. What I feel like is a guy trying to spear a live salmon with a piece of string.

"How can I get her to calm down?" I ask Sally, who is a very patient, older woman from Missouri.

"Don't comfort her. Keep smiling. Be positive. Just give her a job to do and get on with it."

Later, during the afternoon session, Mary Jo comes up to us while we are still struggling alone against the wall, watches for a while, and says:

"You need to have more energy and purpose, Marty. You need to have a purpose for your dog to have a purpose. They mirror you exactly."

"Why is she so hysterical? She's not like this at home," I lie.

"She's upset. She's afraid. I'll bet she's got a high flight drive. She wants to run away."

Ditto.

THAT NIGHT, we drive like twenty miles through a tunnel of winding darkness to a strip mall somewhere that looks like it has just seen the vast zombie invasion, and I try to get my sponsor, Clark, on the phone.

But I hit the wrong speed-dial and am surprised to hear Gloria's voice ask me, "Are you lost?"

"I wish," I say, thinking fast. I'd e-mailed her about the camp, in case something happened. "We made it to the dog camp. It's horrible. I want to leave. It's so confusing. Hola's a mess."

"Now listen," she says. "This is not Harvard Business School. It's a vacation. Calm down."

"It's too advanced. We're not smart enough."

I hear some suspicious crunching noises on her end of the phone.

"What are you doing?" I say. "Are you eating?"

"Doritos. So how do you think Hola's doing?"

"She's the worst dog here."

"Don't you think everyone feels that way?"

"Yes," I say. "Everyone feels like Hola is the worst dog here."

Let loose the hounds of laughter. If it's hysterical, we say in recovery, it's historical. Then I realize Gloria isn't joining me. "Sorry," I say. "It's been a long—"

"Just remember," Gloria says, "you're in partnership with a special-needs dog. This is hard for her. She needs a lot of help. Give it another day."

Then she's gone.

That night I look over from my Susan Conant novel with exhausted eyes at Hola, airplaned on the empty bed next to mine, and say, "What do you say, girl? You want to go back to New York?"

*Z*ʐʐʐʐʐ ʐʐʐʐʐ.

"We can pack it in now, Schmoe. No guilt or regrets. At least for you."

Grrrmmgggg ʐʐʐʐʐ.

She kicks her legs out in her sleep and curls herself into a big ball, her nose resting on the white tip of her tail.

"You want to give it one more day, huh?"

Z_ZZZZZ.

Zzzzz.

CHAPTER EIGHTEEN

Personality

NEXT DAY WE'RE GATHERED in the cellar and a new teacher, Francie, a red-faced woman with a brace of champion agility Jack Russells, announces, "We're going to take a personality test."

"But we did that yesterday," I say. "My dog is high in flight and pack."

"This is not for your dog this time," she says. "It's for you."

Kelly leans into me and whispers, "They want to let the dogs sleep in."

"No," says Stella, "they need time to set up the agility course."

"Maybe," I say, "they want us to learn something."

"Well," snorts Sister Irene, digging her fist deep into the bowl of peanut M&M's. "You're obviously new around here."

So Francie spends an hour explaining the Keirsey Bates and Myers-Briggs personality inventories which are, as promised, for humans.

We take and self-score the inventories, and it turns out I'm semi-introverted, prefer harmony to disagreement, make rapid decisions based on internal rules, and, despite what Sister Irene suspects, have a pessimistic view of the world. I am both sociable and afraid—desperately wanting to belong to the group but scared of everybody in it. If I were a dog, I'd be called high in both pack and flight drives.

In other words, I have the same personality as Hola.

I'm sitting at the table marveling over this coincidence in the half-hour break before class when the woman I'd met on the hill with the Swissies, the tired-looking fortysomething CGC graduate, sits down next to me and says, "How did you do?"

"I'm an INTJ," I say. "I'm doomed."

"So am I," she says. "My name is Beryl."

"It's amazing we're talking, since we're both so introverted.'"

"And afraid."

"Well, actually I'm almost tied on everything, except judgmental. I'm very judgmental."

"I'll be the judge of that."

We talk about our dogs and then she says, "I have a severely autistic son. He's a lot of work. I was kind of losing it, and my husband said I could come to this camp to get away. I needed a break."

"Wow," I say. "This counts as a break? It's stressing me—"

"Are you kidding me? The hills and the . . . the countryside . . . even the no TV—it's such a relief. And my boys are doing so great."

"You can talk to your kids?"

"No" she says, "my Swissies. They're brothers."

I'm awkwardly me-like for a moment, and then Beryl betrays that almost uncanny perceptiveness I've learned to expect from real dog people.

"You know," she says, touching my arm, "I saw you in the class today. You guys are doing fine. Don't wish she was somebody else. They are what they are, you know?"

That night I take an exhausted Hola on a slow walk through a darkening forest, over ruts in the track from horses and ATVs.

We look up at the clouds so close I can almost touch them, and I receive a wordless message from HP.

I need to stop wishing my dog is something else.

I need to stop wishing I was someone else.

This feels like just the first step of the first awakening.

But still, it's the first.

AFTER THAT, we get a little better in class; I'm not sure why. Certainly, neither of us got smarter overnight.

But I'm in the circle as we practice our heel, sit, heel, sit, stand, and heel over and over again, and I notice that Hola has a couple of entirely successful circuits in a row.

And I realize I am not focusing on her, or on myself, but simply feeling how lucky I am to be in a place where everyone is gathered for such a noble cause.

Mary Jo notices our progress, too.

"Look at this dog," she says to the entire class. "You're doing a lot better, Marty. Mind coming in the middle here and showing the group? Remember how much they struggled in the beginning. Now watch how much stiller Marty's upper body is. He's a lot calmer. Have her sit."

We're in the middle of the circle now, the demo team, and I say to Hola, calmly: "Sit."

Nothing.

"Hola, sit."

She stares at me as though I'd asked her to yodel.

Awkward shifting.

"Don't worry," says Mary Jo. "You're gonna learn more from that dog than any you'll ever own. She's just so sensitive.

You have to be very careful with your posture. You all saw how Marty was leaning slightly forward?"

Nods all around: Yup.

"Some dogs it's not so critical, but with Hola here, you can't be casual. She's the most sensitive dog in this room. And that's saying a lot."

As I slouch back into the circle and start up the heeling patterns—my nemesis suddenly remembers how to sit—I'm struck in the face again by how little I actually know my best friend.

And the curriculum gets metaphysically difficult, incredibly fast. A flavor pill for you: day three, we're introduced to the "Stay."

I am proud of Hola's stay now; it is one of her more solid exercises. But this new curve conforms to the Volhards' inability to do things anybody else's way. For the best of behavioral reasons, no doubt, they take your textbook stay and morph it into something by Hieronymus Bosch.

Like this:

Stand next to the dog facing forward in control position with the leash in your right hand curled up with left hand holding up the slack with no dangling ends for Prey drive, and ask your dog to sit with a slight up down pull. When the dog is sitting lower yourself onto your left knee facing forward; the dog is still sitting, you're holding the leash up in your left hand over the dog's head. Reach over with the right hand without leaning into the dog to excite flight defense and put the right forefinger into the collar under the chin, place the left hand over the dog's head and move it straight out like cleaning a bar counter and say: "Stand." Quickly put your left hand under the dog's stomach and raise the dog, keeping the right hand under the buckle. Let go, face forward, and very, very slowly stand up with an erect posture facing forward. Ask the dog to "STAY" and pivot out in front, face forward, count to ten, pivot back, praise the dog but not too loudly and no petting, just an acknowledgment of a job completed and release with "OKAY," running forward with a happy voice, and a tight left circle about turn to transition to Pack drive. Come back to control position, ask your dog to sit at your left, face forward and "Stay."

You lost me at woof.

Hola sleeps like a dead dog on the carpet in front of the door, and I have a very strange dream as I lie shivering in the dark half listening to my girl snore.

I am walking up a thickly wooded mountain with Hola. The vegetation looks like southern Massachusetts. Dense mats of pine needles and browning leaves make a slick path, and I lose my footing at times as I struggle to keep up with Hola, who is strapped into her Sense-ation harness, weaving nervously through a bewildering maze of routes.

The leaves are slippery, and I hear rain drizzling overhead. I look behind me, a steep descent into a rocky river, and there is Hola, as the sun falls and the storm clouds crash into place, frantically trying to help me find the way out.

I wake up a lot more tired than I was when I got into bed.

Hola is now sleeping on top of the bed, in the spot where Gloria should be.

Dog camp graduation.

CHAPTER NINETEEN

Bottom Envy

IF YOU WANT TO KNOW what people are thinking about you, the answer is: seldom.

Which is why I have to call Clark after Hola and I get back from dog camp and ask if he will meet me at a huge Sunday beginners meeting on Eighty-seventh Street. Beginners meetings—designated with a *B* in the meeting lists—are mainly for people who are new to the program or coming back after a relapse. The tone is raw and rugged. Grown men sob out loud. Nobody believes in God. So in the hidden language of our order, simply by saying the name of the meeting, I have already told Clark that the camp did not go particularly well and that I can no longer handle the Gloria thing.

He shows up in his usual khaki pants and rugby shirt, looking slightly tousled, with his round rimless glasses lowering on his ski-slope nose and a baked-in, just-woke-up vibe. I wonder if his kids are keeping him up nights.

The speaker is a well-put-together Wall Street–type woman who's been in and out of the rooms for years. She says something I have often replayed in my head:

"I didn't call people when I needed help," she says. "I thought I was being considerate. I didn't want to bother them. But when did I ever care if I was bothering anybody? No, it's not that at all. I just didn't want to ask for help. I lacked humility."

She looks at me, or near me, saying: "Be humble. Ask for help."

We walk over to the New World Diner on Broadway with a couple of other friends from the morning meeting. Karole is what used to be called a "dark study": blond, late thirties, a successful account executive with a major ad agency, formerly a cokehead so legendary in her West End Avenue co-op that the doormen called her Elvira after the Michelle Pfeiffer character in *Scarface*. To be honest, she scares me: the essence of New York style. In contrast, Darryl is a soft-spoken criminal lawyer with a rigid body and crew-cut silver hair, military in his manner, although he skipped Vietnam for law school and skipped most of law school for the gay scene in Ithaca.

The air is damper than last night, embracing us in its cool plastic arms, and I try to stay here, with these people, not back at camp or home safe in my kennel with Hola.

"Good meeting," I say.

"I used to work with that woman," says Clark.

"The speaker?"

"She was one of the top twenty M and A bankers in the city ten years ago. I wondered what happened to her."

"Now you know."

After we order our crap in the diner, I remember something Darryl said once in a meeting:

"When people ask me what I do for a living, I say, 'As little as possible.' And when they ask me what's my legacy to the world going to be, I say, 'Surviving myself.' "

Brilliant.

"Hey," says Karole, sucking incongruously on a chocolate milkshake in the middle of winter, "how can you tell if an addict is lying?"

"His lips are moving," says Darryl.

I'm studying Karole wrapping her own lips determinedly around the straw, and I say: "I couldn't really eat when I was hungover. The only thing was vanilla milkshakes. I gained thirty pounds my last year out."

Clark says, "At least you got some milk. All I ate was toast and, like, Froot Loops right out of the box—"

Darryl: "That's something solid anyway. I lived on vodka for a year. Everything else came right back up the way it went down."

Karole: "I remember a month I ate nothing but cocaine."

Me: "You ate it?"

Karole: "You know what I mean. I wish I could have kept down some carbs."

Me: "What did you weigh?"

Karole: "Eighty-five pounds."

Darryl: "Ouch."

Karole: "You lost your woody, huh?"

Clark: "The fourth or fifth time I was in the locked ward, the nurse there said, 'Sir, hate to tell you this; you've got the heart, lungs, and kidneys of a ninety-year-old man on life support.' And I'm like, 'Where is he? I'll give 'em back!' "

Me: "You're kidding, right?"

Clark: "I wish—"

Darryl: "Ninety—hah! In my dreams. When I was in the ICU, Cedars Sinai, I heard later they gave me a fifty-fifty chance to live."

Karole: "There were times I wished I had fifty-fifty. After my second DWI, I passed out in the back of the cop car; they're taking me to the county jail in Little Rock. They call the EMT, guy takes one look at me, and says, 'She's dead.' "

Me: "You made that up—"

Karole: "I bought blow from the guy later. He told me."

Me: "So you're, what, a zombie?"

Clark: "My last time, I collapsed on the sidewalk outside Hooters. I'm lying in a pool of blood and shit; they can't find my ID. So I'm a John Doe in the Bellevue ER, and they're like, 'This guy's obviously a homeless derelict; let's not treat him.' "

Darryl: "Sad."

Karole: "I was left in a back room, some Mexican motel one time. These guys said they had some meth, but they just took me to this place to fuck. So I'm so drunk I pass out, don't know what happens. I wake up, there's blood everywhere, and I'm naked; everything's gone."

Darryl: "At least you were over eighteen. I was fifteen; one time, I'm at a porno movie with my rabbi, and he's feeding me these pills and Southern Comfort, and I'm like, 'Abba, I feel really weird,' and he's like—"

Karole: "Wait! Can I call too much information here? Please."

Darryl: "Sorry."

Karole: "I'm sorry for you."

An awkward pause. Darryl puts two French fries in his nostrils and laughs. Then he stops. Silence.

Me: "Anybody see the *Real Housewives* last night?"

Karole: "That show is so fake."

When we first get sober, for a while we wish our story wasn't so bad. It embarrasses us. But after we get a little more time in the program, most of us start wishing our stories were much worse. In the inverted universe of recovery, the most dramatic stories—the nearest near-death experiences—are the ones that get the most respect. It is a strange but very real phenomenon we call Bottom Envy.

And it's the reason why this conversation, so shocking to an outsider, actually cheers me up a lot. We're just people being people. Is everything my friends said absolutely true?

Like Darryl said, their lips were moving.

Clark and I linger a while after the other two leave to put their respective children and pets to bed, and I ask him if he's okay.

"You seem pensive tonight," I observe. "Kind of tired."

"Oh, you know, work."

"What work?" I look at him: his left hand is shaking very slightly as it lifts his coffee cup, and his eyes are rimmed black as though he hasn't slept in days. "You're rich and successful and all that—I know—but I have no idea what you actually do all day. Where's your office?"

"And how's Hola hanging? How was camp?"

"Are you changing the subject on me?"

He's fingering his plate of cold onion rings, worrying one of them like it's a wedding band.

"Can I make a suggestion?" he says.

"Huh?"

"You need to set a date."

"For what?"

"For this Canine Good Citizen thing. Stop putzing around. Pick a day you're going to do it and do it. Tell everyone—tell Gloria—and just do it."

"What if we fail?"

"It doesn't matter," he says. "Taking this test is an estimable act. It's how you build your credibility back with Gloria. You need to build it back."

"By failing in public?"

"You're missing the point here," he says. "You need to start making real commitments, announcing them to everybody, and then—the important thing here—actually doing them. I guarantee you Gloria will be impressed no matter what happens."

"What if she shows up? Watches us screw up?"

"That's the whole idea, genius. You *want* her to show up."

I think about this scheme of Clark's; it seems kind of flawed to me. *Estimable acts.* What? Meanwhile, he steeples his fingers under his chin, an onion ring still wrapped around his wedding finger.

"Can I make another suggestion?" he says.

"No."

"And I promise this is not a selfish, manipulative thing on my part. Though maybe it is."

"Huh?"

"How do you feel about cats?"

CHAPTER TWENTY

Ruby the Cat

A FEW MONTHS EARLIER, when Gloria was sick in bed with a cold, I thought she was sufficiently weakened to give me permission to do something I'd wanted to do for years: get a cat.

So I told her about my cat dream, while she was blowing her nose, and she said: "What?"

"I'd like a cat. She can be a friend for Hola. You know, during the day. And maybe Hola can mentor her, show her the—"

"You're getting a pet for our dog?"

"Well, not exactly. More like a . . . a protégé."

"You're insane."

"It will be fun," I said, weakly. "More animals around."

Luckily for me, Gloria's illness ensured she was not quite so formidable an adversary as she would normally have been.

"I cannot take care of this cat," she said. "It's your idea."

"No problem. I'll do it."

"You ever had a cat—*achoo*—before?"

"When I was a kid. GP. He wasn't fixed. Impregnated the whole neighborhood. He came back scratched up sometimes. He was quite the womanizer. It was the seventies."

"GP? What's that stand for?"

"General Practitioner."

"Of course."

Momentarily at a loss, benumbed and bewildered, she dabbed

her red nose with a wad of soft tissue. Then offered, randomly: "Dogs are more popular than cats."

"Meaning?"

"You never hear about a cat pulling kids out of a burning building. Cats never get sent into the snow to rescue people. Nobody has a cat leading them around the city or ub and down stairs. Cats don't join the army or the FBI or protect our borders from egsblosives. You want to know why cats aren't as bopular as dogs?"

"Not really."

"Because they don't *do* anything."

"That's not you talking," I said. "It's the flu."

"Neber mind," she said. "I need to tabe a nab. *Achoo.*"

As I left her there in the dark, I thought I heard a prophetic, subverbal muttering. It sounded something like:

"I hobe she liges Hola."

The weekend after our late-night "Bottom Envy" session at the New World Diner on Broadway, I meet Clark outside his apartment building on the Upper West Side in the shadow of Roosevelt Hospital, and he hands me an aqua-colored cat box with a wailing little critter inside.

"I wish I could keep her," he says, a little unconvincingly, "but my wife has bad allergies."

"Is she always this noisy?"

"Oh, no," he says. "Just when she's hungry."

What he fails to tell me is that—much like her bigger stepsister Hola—she is always hungry.

"What's her name?" I ask him.

"Miss Ruby. You can call her Ruby." I should have smelled trouble: already, the cat's handing out permissions.

So I take the wailing cat box, say a regretful thank-you to Clark, and head to Columbus Avenue to look for a cab.

I still don't know if Ruby likes Hola, but the two of them certainly keep me amused. They have been from the beginning like an operetta in the key of wow, dramatic and silly by turns, and enormously loud.

The Curtain Rises:

RUBY: I was not overly impressed by the human when he appeared outside my caretaker's home. I told him as much through the holes in my jail. He moved me into a little room with the moving walls and the songs on the radio that use only a very small part of the audible spectrum. I'm screaming as we leave the room and get cold and warm again. He seems annoyed by me.

Note to humans: if we're hissing at you, you probably deserve it.

We enter the region this big man obviously lives in. His kennel. I can tell because it smells like him—terrible. He takes me out of the jail and holds me incorrectly. Not supporting me underneath. What a yahoo. Meanwhile, I need to do whatever it takes to get under that sofa.

Ahhhh.

What's that?!!

A monster!

An enormous black hairy beast! God, it's big. I've never seen anything like it. And that gleam in its eye—it's obviously hungry—the saliva. Shit. They're going to feed me to it. These people are barbarians.

A short while later:

Oh.

Okay.

I'm in the back.

There's a set of bars up—and the monster's on the other side. They leave me in peace. Wonderful. I'm probably on deck for the pagan rituals.

HOLA: What is it!? A little dog in a cage. I must liberate her! Dad has imprisoned the little dog. She seems afraid of something. I must help her overcome her fear.

God, am I hungry. These humans are starving me. What? I forgot what I was saying. What a big day. There's Dad's shoe. I'm going to take this into the bedroom where it belongs. For my nap.

What would these people do without me to pick up after them?

RUBY *(a few days later):* The human has let me live, for now. I talk to him, but he only knows how to mumble. That's why I stay behind this radiator. I've been here for days. It's actually quite warm.

The mise en scène of this place is more tidy and congenial than my last human's. He was not very good with details. Nor was he obedient. This person has some potential. If only I could find some way to get rid of the monster.

I think it's time I introduced him to the new boss.

HOLA: Every morning I'm up. First thing: the little dog. I run into the back room. She hides behind the radiator. I'm bowing and sniffing. Practically doing backflips to show her I'm friendly. What more does she want? An engraved bag of poop. I'll give it to her. What was I saying?

God, I'm starved. Dad is turning me into a stick. It's so unfair.

I love that little dog so much. She's so strange. Probably doesn't make friends easily. Not a problem. Maybe some wrestling. A few rounds of Whac-a-Mole. I feel like we're sisters.

Dad's back! Maybe if I stand here and do that eye-batting thing, he'll give me some Swiss Emmentaler. He always does. His training is coming along. Though lately he's forgetting more. Where was I?

Ruby lets her pets relax.

I return from church one day to find Ruby asleep in the middle of Hola's doggie bed.

And Hola herself, enawed, airplaned out on the floor in front of the bed staring up at her new master.

Miss Ruby has assumed her throne.

Order sings out from the chaos, and the sun is released by the sea.

Unbelievable, really. The cat who is one-tenth Hola's size and 5 percent as big as I am has established her dominance over the dog. She owns the space around her. Commands the higher plateaus.

It's embarrassing. Mainly for me.

CHAPTER TWENTY-ONE

Working Dog

THE FOLLOWING WEEK, during my annual performance review at my job, I find myself getting the same feedback I've been enjoying since I left business school a decade ago. I used to be outraged; then I thought they may be on to something; now I know that they are.

Smart people get sober, too. It just takes them longer.

Trouble is, the review is delivered in a forceful—well, belligerent—style by my new division head, Huxley. The menschy, squeezable Don, who hired me and kept me through my bottom and early sobriety, who once alluded to knowing I was in the program and seemed to approve, moved to LA. His replacement was like an ironic commentary on Don: short, swarthy, high-voiced, volatile, extraordinarily hyper, a torrent of opinions and abuse.

Which brings me to my performance review. Huxley's office is as warm as he is: nothing on the walls except a whiteboard and calendar with key deliverable dates; a desktop oddly uncluttered except by a phone, pen and paper, my review, a cactus, and a framed picture of an unattractive, undersized dachshund. My review, I notice, is lying next to the cactus.

"So," he starts, "I got some feedback." After what sounds to me like an obligatory sprint through the positives, he gets to it: "There's one area you can work on."

"Yes?"

He looks at me directly, parts all ten of his fingers and jabs them at me: "We need you to man up, Marty."

"What?"

"You back down too much. We need to hear your opinion—push back more. Argue with the people on the team. You're always so nice and reasonable."

"Is that bad?"

"It makes me uncomfortable."

" . . . ?"

"I don't care if we all get along," he says. "I care if we all get it right. The ideal meeting to me is like two carbs fighting in a bowl. You know what I'm saying?"

I say, "Carbs?"

"What?"

"You said 'carbs fighting in a bowl.' How does that work?"

"I mean crabs—you know what I mean. Speak up! You hearing me?"

Dogs rely more on sound than on sight. I am hearing his sound loud enough. I'm wondering, *Should I push back on it? Is this a test?*

"What if I don't disagree?" I ask.

"That's not the point," he says. "Disagree anyway. It's a process."

"How does that help get to the right answer?"

"It does if you're right."

"Right?"

"Right."

"I'm lost."

"Give you an example," he says. "Look at"—here, he mentions one of the most egregious bitches I have the misfortune to work alongside. "She tells people what she thinks. She'll push back a lot."

"Ah."

"Why are you smiling? This is serious."

"I know it is," I say, sincerely. "It's just, I'm looking at that picture of your dog. Cute little guy."

Huxley lowers his hands, settles back in his chair, and lets out a contented breath, beaming.

"That's my Andy," he says. "Two years old. Awesome dog."

"How are his manners?"

"Perfect. I put him in a down during dinner; he sits right under the table and doesn't move."

"For how long?"

"Like, I don't know, an hour. He's amazing."

"Did he come that way?"

He shakes his head, then cradles it in his hands and leans even farther back, looking like Hola when she's getting a tummy rub.

"He was horrible at first," he says. "Barked all the time. Guarded things. Couldn't handle separation. Between you and me, I couldn't control him. I had like ten pounds of dog pushing me around. It was humiliating."

"Wolves and dogs try to avoid conflicts," says Norwegian trainer Turid Rugaas. "They are conflict-solving animals. It is usually we, the human species, who tend to create conflicts between our dogs and ourselves."

"What did you do?" I ask Huxley.

"Got an amazing trainer. Did the homework."

Bingo. "Can I get a name from you?"

That night I tell Clark about the feedback at work, its pushy regularity. He tells me he can't talk long because he and his wife are expecting some of their incredibly wealthy, gorgeous friends over for dinner, and he has to hand tie his bow tie.

"Here's what you say," he says to me. "Next time, you say, 'You want my *opinion*? You guys are full of shit! How's that for an *opinion!* Hah!' "

I'm laughing now. Perspective inches back.

"Oh, my God," I choke out. "Totes."

"What did you say?"

"Totes."

"I heard some guy say that on a call today. *Totes.* What the fuck does it mean?"

Hola cranes her neck around and looks at me from a caustic angle, then shakes her head rapidly from side to side, ears fluttering like an asynchronous bird of prey before her chin alights gently on my kneecap. Ruby then hurls herself off the chair cushion and flounces off in the direction of the kitchen with her tail erect, yowling:

"Ik ik ik YOOOOUUUWW."

CHAPTER TWENTY-TWO

Dog Training

ORGANIZED OBEDIENCE competitions appeared in America in the 1930s, driven largely by a standard poodle breeder named Helene Whitehouse Walker, who toured dog clubs to evangelize dog training as a sport. Walker ran the first obedience event, with eight dogs, in Mount Kisco, New York, in 1933. Train Your Dog became a Depression-era slogan, and by 1936 the AKC had published its first competition regulations.

Soon Walker was joined in her demo wagon by Blanche Saunders, who became the godmother of obedience for decades and, in the 1950s, published the first modern guidebook for trainers. Her methods were typical of the time: no food, but you could praise; look for the dog to do something wrong and jerk on a choke chain around his neck; use physical guidance to teach things like sits.

Although basically humane, Saunders was part of an ancestral chain that ran from the ancient Romans through the nineteenth century, when it was believed that dogs, like children and horses, needed to be "broken," and that, in the words of a popular manual published in 1894, "All knowledge not beaten into a dog is worthless for all practical purposes."

Animal behaviorists call this method—correcting errors with aversive consequences—negative reinforcement. The most notorious of the negative gurus was William Koehler, head of training for Walt Disney Studios and the man behind the dog actors in *Swiss Family Robinson* and *The Incredible Journey*, among many others. His book, *The Koehler Method of Dog Training*, was the best-selling obedience title in the United States for decades.

Today, it can make for terrifying reading:

"Hold [the dog] suspended until he has neither the strength nor inclination to renew the fight," he writes. "Once lowered he will probably stagger loop-legged for a few steps, vomit once or twice, and roll over on his side. But do not let it alarm you."

Koehler believed in nipping problems in the bud with a massive display of pain. Training was a battle of wills, and it was you or the dog. Yet he had a good heart: he honestly believed it was actually hurtful to be too kind and that the greatest of all physical and psychological cruelties was—ready now?—"under-correction."

A popular medical textbook from 1907 describes how alcoholics were routinely treated:*

"When an alcoholic called for [the doctor], he immediately placed the patient upon the operating table, introduced the stomach tube, pumped out the stomach, then washed it out, and after he had freed the stomach of all mucous and contents, he gave the patient a bowl of hot essence of capsicum, and allowed him to rest for a few hours."

Conclusion: "Perhaps the rapid, cruel treatment . . . may be the most humane after all."

Well into the 1970s, drunks were routinely locked up in asylums, strapped to tables, force-fed belladonna, castor oil, and stewed tomatoes, and subjected to therapy sessions that were little more than moralistic bullying.

---

*George Barton Cutten, *The Psychology of Alcoholism*.

Clinical psychologists are still conducting experiments into modalities such as "emetic and electric shock alcohol aversion therapy"*—a *Clockwork Orange*-esque attempt to make them nauseous at the sight of alcohol.

Starting in the late 1970s—when, some might point out, former hippies started getting dogs for their kids—things shifted. "Like human therapies, for the most part dog training has undergone an evolution and moved toward a more positive approach," write animal behaviorists Mary Burch and Jon Bailey in *How Dogs Learn*.

Positive methods include clicker training, promoted by the dolphin expert Karen Pryor, a more precise way to tell the animal which behavior you are actually rewarding. From what they've done wrong to what they've done right, it's an approach that works well for most dogs, who are basically easygoing and eager to please, because that's the kind of dog we humans have been selectively breeding for centuries.

But growling and snapping; lunging at other dogs; yanking us down the street; refusing to surrender things they've got in their mouth; tackling old ladies who smile in the elevator and breaking a hip, leading to lawsuits, evictions, homelessness, and jail . . . Even if it doesn't go that far, there are limits to the power of a hot dog when some real dogs crave excitement in their lives.

The so-called click-and-treat method dominated dog training for a generation. And then came Cesar Millan. His TV show, *The Dog Whisperer*, has been seen by 50 million people on the National Geographic Channel—and there are only about 65 million dogs in the United States. This former illegal immigrant

Journal of Consulting and Clinical Psychology 49 (1981): 360–68.

from Sinaloa, Mexico, is a $100 million industry, with leadership seminars, books, DVDs, and pet food.

He doesn't use a clicker and rarely pulls out a treat. His credo is that dogs need a leader, the leader is you, and they must be given this information by any means necessary.

Anti–Cesar Millanism is epidemic in the pet dog training world, at least in the Northeast, and it comes out in ways that are sometimes pretty funny. My club, the Port Chester Obedience Training Club, gives all its students a recommended reading list. Along with books by Ian Dunbar and Karen Pryor are newer feel-good classics such as Andrea Arden's *Dog-Friendly Dog Training* and Joel Walton's *Positive Puppy Training Works*. And under a title by Paul Owens called *The Dog Whisperer*, they emphasize: "(NOT to be confused with the book with the same title written by Cesar Milan)."

Whom they hate too much even to spell his name right.

An op-ed columnist in the *New York Times* recently called Millan "a charming, one-man wrecking ball directed at 40 years of progress in understanding and shaping dog behavior."

Millan talks about observing the dogs on his grandfather's farm as a boy, how they would fight among themselves until a clear leader emerged, at which point peace reigned in the pack. He likens them to wild wolf packs, which were long thought to be held together by a dominant "alpha male."

But as animal behaviorists have been quick to point out, our pet dogs are not wolves—far from it. Cats are behaviorally much closer to wild cats than domestic dogs are to wolves. Fifteen millennia of coevolution have changed dogs to such an extent that they cannot survive without us. We have turned them into our own better halves.

To take just one example, the reason dogs bark so much is

because we talk. Wild animals rarely vocalize; their communication is visual and olfactory. But humans are verbal, and so we've proactively anthropomorphized this trait into our dogs. And dogs are the only animal that can naturally follow where a human is pointing or looking; even chimpanzees cannot do this.

Interestingly, aversive training methods do not work well on wild animals. A wild animal will literally fight a human to death rather than *not* do what we punish him for. Dogs are different: we have taught them to submit to pain.

And so on.

Dominance is a complicated topic, but more recent work on wolves in the wild, including a multiyear study by L. David Mech on northwestern Canada's Ellesmere Island, seems to show that packs function more like families than conscripted armies: they accept roles rather than take them by force.

As animal behaviorist Temple Grandin says, "What dogs probably need isn't a substitute *pack leader* but a substitute *parent*." Either way, though, the human should be setting the tone.

Among serious dog trainers, as opposed to pet owners, the anti-Millan feeling is much less pronounced. "I've got to give Cesar credit," Wendy Volhard told us at dog camp. "He takes on behavior problems that the rest of us wouldn't touch."

As Millan himself takes pains to point out, "I *don't 'train'* dogs." What he means is that he corrects behavior problems; if your dog isn't having serious issues, Millan is not your man.

Having been primed for the worst, I was surprised as I made my way through Millan's book, written with Melissa Jo Peltier, called *Be the Pack Leader*. It made a lot of sense: "We've gone from the old-fashioned authoritarian extreme—where animals existed only to do our bidding—to another unhealthy extreme—where animals are considered our equal partners in every area of our lives."

I thought of dog writer Jon Katz's observation that "as a Boomer parent in a child-centric town, I'd spent years watching people struggle to say no to their kids and their dogs."

Millan talks less about forcing dogs to do our bidding than reshaping *ourselves* to be worthy of our dogs' respect, by becoming confident people who exude what he calls "a calm-assertive energy."

In an article about Millan a few years ago, writer Malcolm Gladwell quoted the well-known canine ethologist Patricia McConnell: "I believe [dogs] pay a tremendous amount of attention to how relaxed our face is and how relaxed our facial muscles are, because that's a big cue for them with each other. Is the jaw relaxed? Is the mouth slightly open? And then the arms. They pay a tremendous amount of attention to where our arms go."

Or, as Millan himself says: "Dogs know how comfortable you are with yourself, how happy you are, how fearful you are, and what is missing inside of you."

Putting down his book, I can only think: *Oops.*

CHAPTER TWENTY-THREE

Barkbuster

THE SMALL WOMAN in the camo T-shirt and parachute pants makes a quick scan of my battered chew-toy sofa and Hola's worn-out chaise lounge from Domain.

"Obviously," she says, "the dog has furniture privileges."

"Don't all dogs?" I ask her.

"No," she sniffs. "They do not."

Although I have her on leash, Hola is trying to catapult herself off her new friend's breasts when the woman makes a sound I've never heard from a human being before: "*Grrrrrggghhgg.*"

Deep, guttural, sharp, disarming: the sound of a dog backing up against a flaming wall.

Like magic, Hola plants four on the floor, lowers her head and her tail, and steps back.

"Sit," says the woman, calm-assertively.

Hola sits.

This, I'm thinking, has potential.

I'd found this woman, who changed my life, by asking the most dominant person I knew—namely, my boss—who had helped him train his dog. That his dog was a tiny dachshund just made his good manners more rare: these rodents are usually wretched because nobody fears them enough to even bother.

"Her name is Lorena," he'd said. "She will change your life."

"Does she use a clicker?"

"A what?"

Lorena has the kind of full-blooded New York accent—*dawgs uv got they-uh own lang-wage*—you don't hear so much anymore, blunt-cut straight red hair and copious freckles on an open oval face like an overgrown kid's. She's not too clean-looking, like a woman who spends her time with canines and bad men. Of course, she's chewing gum—or thumbtacks.

I'm sitting on my bomb-zone sofa with Hola at my side listening to her say:

"The problem is, people don't know how to communicate with their dogs. We need to learn their language. See the world from their point of view. They have one job and that job is to train us. We're a lot more important to them than they are to us, if you think about it. They don't have a lot of other options."

Regaining her charm after a temporary setback, Hola starts testing Lorena: poking, nuzzling at her, probing her knees.

"She does a lot of attention-seeking behavior," Lorena points out. "Demands to get petted and so on. Does a whole lotta that."

" 'Cause she's pretty," she says, "she gets a lot of attention. It works for her. I bet it's worse with men—big men, right?"

"How did you know?"

"That's your fault; you trained her. She bats her eyes, rubs against you—you pet her and talk to her. She doesn't really care if you yell at her or praise her. The point is she's training you. Meaning she gives the cue, you do the thing."

Hola rolls over onto her back.

Lorena smiles for the first time since she got here.

"This is her pulling out everything she's got," she says, BB-ing her eyes into mine. "You pet her right now, I'm gonna have to kill you."

"Dogs need a boss," she says after a second. "Somebody's the leader. Most of them want it to be you. It's like the military—if there's no leader, people are going to die. That's the way they think. It's not like people—we talk; everybody contributes, you know. More like children—that's their mentality. Think about two-year-olds—how they think. You can't keep feeding them candy all the time, right? Don't answer that.

"Dogs get dominance through height. Not necessarily taller breeds—within the breeds. That's why she gets up on furniture. Why she jumps up on people. When she jumps up, she's higher. Telling people she's dominant from the beginning. Thought she was being friendly, right? Dogs may have a tendency but will go to both dominant and submissive from time to time. Your girl probably does both."

Momentarily flummoxed, Hola heaves herself to standing and starts to oscillate slowly back and forth between us, like a furry washing machine.

"Hola, sit," she says, and Hola does, skyrocketing right back up like the floor is on fire.

"I think she's naturally submissive, believe it or not," Lorena says, amazing me. "This is not a particularly dominant dog. I can tell. This dog should not be all that hard to train."

Off my wilted-lettuce look: "Sorry, Marty. You thought you had a Bernese Marley, right—and what you really got here is a Taco Bell."

My phone vibrates, and I check who it is. Not Gloria. I had caved in to Clark's advice and set a date for our Canine Good Citizen test: December 19. Less than one month away. I had e-mailed the date, time, and place to Gloria, and she hadn't responded. Now I feel like I'm sitting through a sad animal movie—which is basically every animal movie—and I don't know why.

"We're not going to use treats anymore for training," Lorena says. "It doesn't work for telling them what you *don't* want them to do. Jumping on people is so much better than any treat. You have to keep raising the treat ante. So what are you, going to have a piece of filet mignon out there? Caviar?"

"So what do we do?" I ask her.

"It's simple," she says and proceeds to lay out our new method:

From now on, Hola doesn't get anything she wants unless she does something in return.

First.

Not just food, but anything she wants: petting, a walk, dinner, furniture time. She sits before every door, every flight of stairs, every exit or entrance. She doesn't move until I say, "Okay."

"And how do I get her to do this?" I ask, getting testy.

"Just like this," she says.

"Sit," she says to Hola, and as Hola hesitates, she growls "*Grrrrgggh!*" and snaps gently on the leash.

Hola sits.

"Good dog!" she sings, happily. "Very good girl."

"The thing most people forget," says Lorena, "is to praise dogs when they do it right. No treat, just praise. You want voice control of your animal. It's more important than the correction. Ideally, you want to get to a place where you're praising all the time and don't need the growl."

"But for now . . ." I say.

"The growl."

This new Lorena Method is certainly a lot easier than the

Port Chester Obedience Training Club protocol, logistically. I don't have to fumble with clickers and treats and so on, which I never quite mastered. As Lorena had said, a food-motivated dog will do anything for a treat. It's a monologue, not a dialogue.

If I have a treat in my possession, Hola will go through a sit, down, stay, backflip, and tarot card reading—all before I have time to give her a command. It becomes: I'll do everything till something works. A kind of Las Vegas school of human behavior modification.

"Our goal," says Lorena, "should be to get them to do something because we asked them to. Good things happen when they do what we say. Annoying things happen to them when they don't. It's as simple as that."

We go around Trinity Church Cemetery, the only active cemetery in Manhattan. It's a Gothic slab of old New York, a steep and rocky lot of ornate gravesites climbing from the West Side Highway to upper Broadway, remnant of a time when Washington Heights looked more like Bern, Switzerland, than a burn ward.

Hola trots along between Lorena and me as we talk, and I'm holding the leash. She's pretty well-behaved, by my standards, but Lorena works from a stricter rule book.

"She's forging ahead," she says. "Use the correction."

"Grrr," I say, self-consciously.

"Hola forges ahead—*Grrr* like a taser, okay?"

I pull Hola back and around until she's at my side.

"There's no sniffing, chewing, whatever, unless you say so," says Lorena. "Her job on the walk is to walk next to you until you tell her to stop. That's her job. Heel position. That's it."

We angle back down Broadway, within sight of the massive Episcopalian cathedral; as usual, as I'm walking Hola between the cemetery and the cathedral spires, I feel as though we are padding softly over a tapestry woven from the spirits of the dead.

Lorena says, "She picks stuff up fast. She obviously wants to please you."

"What?"

"Yeah, that's why she's so fast. She has a lovely temperament. You're lucky. She's smart too."

"We're talking about Hola, right? This dog right down here?"

"What you need is to challenge her more."

We navigate 156th Street past Boricua College and descend the slope to Riverside Drive, and I'm thinking that Hola seems to have mastered the heel: her nose at my kneecap, trotting with her tail a-wag and her head sweeping the antique-brick sidewalk for signs of chicken-related detritus.

Watching her, Lorena says, "This dog is not very dominant, Marty. Why did you say that when you called me?"

"I don't know. I just assumed that was the problem—that she was dominant and she didn't respect me enough."

"She doesn't respect you enough. But it's not because she's alpha."

The Volhards convinced me that Hola was fearful. Now Lorena is saying she's a natural follower. Fearful and submissive is surely not the dog I thought I knew.

Back in the apartment, I practice having her sit-stay while Lorena knocks on the door and comes in like a fake visitor.

This is very hard for Hola.

We break it down into pieces: the knock, turning the doorknob, opening a crack, opening more, Lorena coming in, Lorena saying hello, Lorena shaking my hand.

Each time, Hola's corrected for breaking the stay without waiting for my signal.

"Don't do too much at once," Lorena says. "It's important to make things easy for her. If all your sessions are about failure, it makes you seem weak. Success for her makes you strong. Leadership is about how the world is arranged. Well arranged means good leadership. Hola wants to be with the stronger leader. It's natural. It's just a lot less stress for her."

"Do you like Cesar?" I ask her as she's getting ready to leave.

Her moon-round eyes narrow slightly, as though she's wary of the question, but she's nodding her head.

"Problem with Cesar," she says, "is people see the show, but they're not him. They don't see all the subtle things he's doing—the body language, how he positions himself. Eye contact. It's like a dance, you know. He looks like a magician, and they're not seeing what he's doing. They try it at home and get bit or whatever. But you know, man, it's not the dog's freaking fault."

CHAPTER TWENTY-FOUR

Gift to the Dog

LORENA LEAVES ME with a handout titled "The Rules of Passive Dominance," which begins: "Ignoring attention-seeking behaviors is the highest form of dominance."

The *highest* form?

Attention seeking: Grabbing shoes and making you chase her. Soft sweet cries and I say, "What's wrong, Hola, you hungry, doll?" Poke and pet, roll over and rub reflexively, even yelling "Drop!" when she's got our neighbor's kid's sandal in her mouth, shaking it like a squirrel that's dead enough already.

Negative or positive—it's all attention seeking.

What she lives for.

"Her job is to train you," Lorena had said. "She's better at her job than you are because she is more focused. It's all she thinks about."

Hola's toolbox consists of annoying me until I do what she wants.

Which I always do.

Why?

Because it's annoying, that's why.

And if I don't?

Drama queen.

She'll collapse on the floor like a character in *Gossip Girl* tossing her Fendi bag onto the davenport.

Now I'm seeing her behaviors through a new frame. Her whining isn't an existential scripture on the brevity of life. The way she pokes her head and makes me pet her isn't a rhapsody on the mutability of love.

No, the new hermeneutics is that she's a spoiled kid throwing tantrums just to get her way. The more I look at her I see she is in a state of perpetual tantrum. She makes spoiled kids look evolved.

How can I have been so wrong for so long?

Ignorance is an expensive occupation.

But I don't want to be too hard on myself. I am reading Sharon Chesnutt Smith's classic book on the Bernese mountain dog, and I run across the following passage in her section called "Temperament and Characteristics":

"Bernese like to keep in touch. So just to make sure you are with them, they have a habit of backing up and sitting on their owners' feet. . . . Then there is the 'Berner Bump.' This involves a Bernese sticking its head under your hand or arm and forcefully nudging it until you provide the petting."

What Lorena would call naked displays of dominance and signs of pathological attention seeking are, to Smith, simply the endearing characteristics of a friendly breed.

WHAT I DISCOVER, as I have in the program, is that following instructions can be liberating.

Rules seem like tyranny to the immature, but the greatest tyranny of all is indecision—it is paralysis—and everybody in marketing knows indecision is a consequence more often of too much choice rather than too little.

Every doorway, I make Hola sit and stay. I go through it. Say okay and she follows.

Every doorway. Up and down the stairs. If she doesn't sit, I do what Lorena's leave-behinds called a "check" with the leash, and I make my *Grr* sound.

The noise I make is like a buzzer on a game show when you get the answer wrong. Hola understands right away what it means. It means: "Try again."

Lorena said it's like a growl, instinctively understood, like what mother dogs do to their puppies when they get out of line. The tone is what is important—not the words—for conveying information. Making it clearer to Hola that nothing good is going to happen for her unless she lives by the rules.

What rules?

The rules that I make.

You can't think your way into right living. You have to live your way into right thinking.

All dog trainers say you have to be more patient than your dog. Eventually, it becomes logical to them to get it over with and do what this silly person seems to want. Obedience doesn't hurt—not physically. It's just a kind of inconvenience with a life-saving outcome. Like going to work or making your meetings.

On our walks, I never let her get in front of me. When she breaks heel position, I do my buzzer and the check. She picks it all up right away. In fact, it sort of seems like it's all the same to her: walk up front, walk near me; at least somebody has a point of view.

Without the treats, she is definitely calmer. Focused on the air, the ground, her endless search for something edible, her nonstop recon for another little dog to vote for her.

I am not making this up or imagining things that did not happen when I admit: our relationship changed within a single day.

I don't do anything different. Not really. Just give myself permission to lead.

Dominance is hardly scary—not like I'd imagined. It's not a battle of wills between two armed combatants. It's more like an off-site with HR where people are given new titles and a performance review. The review might be unsettling for a moment or two, but after that, we just act our pay grade; and we are relieved by the routine of knowing where it is that we fit in the organization that allows us to honor our bills.

To the dog, training is like a daily performance review, so it needs to be delivered in the language that they speak.

By leading, we are taking on stress on behalf of our dog. We are assuming responsibility to negotiate the world, especially that part more than one or two feet off the ground. Studies have shown leaders have higher blood pressure than followers. Leaders have more stress hormones in their blood. Despite what business books may tell you, leadership is not the natural state of most people, or dogs. We may not be born to run—but we are usually born to follow.

Our new relationship is expressed in small moments of awareness and intention; I'm aware of what she is doing now every moment of our working time. And a walk is mostly working time. Strong leadership takes vigilance, monitoring, care.

Take it from one who knows well: part of the reason a lot of us want our dogs to be free and not looking to us all the time for instructions is because we cannot be bothered with the alternative.

Being a leader is a *lot* more work—and I don't mean for the dog.

At the door I say, "Sit," and she sits. I walk through. Her caboose leaves the ground before I say okay, it's *Grrr*.

Back.

"Sit." Sit. "Okay."

She follows me through the door.

There are two doors: we do it twice.

There are three stairs beyond the second door.

She sits at the top of the stairs.

I go down the stairs.

Wait.

"Okay."

If she breaks the sit, even if it's just to stand and wait for me, it's *Grrr*.

Go back up the stairs. Sit, stay; go down the stairs.

Wait.

"Okay."

Crossing the lobby requires an immediate heel: "With me!" I say.

Pat my leg with my left hand. Indicating she follows me at heel.

Down. Down-stay. People pass. They smile. She has to stay. Her tail twitches on the marble slabs.

She wants so badly to jump up on these people it's almost like she can taste the salt in their eyes. But no. Okay.

At the elevator, she can't stand and sniff and wait for a dog to appear through the crack in the miracle door. It's a sit, a down, stay, *Grr*, again, stay, *Grr*, repeat, rinse, recycle, remember.

Then again, if you think she's just going to be trotting out through the elevator door on our floor, you haven't been paying attention. It's a wait for me; leaders first.

And the hall. Don't get me started on the hall—ending in a sit outside our door, and as I open it, she stands. Because dinner is inside there somewhere, somehow. But *Grrr*. Nope. Close door, sit again, wait wait wait. Open door. Stand. *Grr*.

Until she waits as it's opened, as I go inside, look into her face, and say the magic word:

"Okay."

Of course she has to sit or down before she gets her dinner bowl.

Not to mention five or ten minutes on the wood flooring of the living room practicing our down-stays—the command she's been forgetting for years.

Hola doesn't like her new trainer.

Now, what is my point in describing all this? To drive you to tears? Send you into the loving arms of Satan?

No, it's this: to ask you to think about what I've just described. Is that how you get your pushy, troublemaking bitch from the front door to the dinner bowl? Well, why not? Lorena isn't teaching us competitive obedience handling here. I'm not getting Hola ready for the show rings or the OTCH trials. What I'm talking about is making a nice, friendly pet.

See what I mean about laziness?

Isn't it more natural for people like us to put up with a little growling in the lobby, a few avoidant neighbors, a nip or two on the leash, for a little freaking freedom of our own?

Because leading your dog, I'm beginning to see, is a job. And it's much more of a gift to the dog than a convenience to the owner.

CHAPTER TWENTY-FIVE

Best Dog Ever

THE MIGHTY BERNESE MOUNTAIN DOG, capstone of canine creation, apex of Mount Woofy, is not, apparently, the perfect pet. According to the AKC's official description, repeated over the PA at televised breed shows such as Westminster, "This is not a breed for everyone."

The AKC boilerplate tends to be written in a kind of soft code, a muted set of pastels instead of vivid colors of truth. Compare that note to the harsh warning officially attached to another notoriously difficult large breed: "Malamutes are great family dogs."

Huh?

In context, "This is not a breed for everyone" means something like: *"Stop, drop and roll, dude! Run and don't look back!"*

Nonetheless, the Berner's Cary Grant–like charm and striking looks, aided by a featured appearance in the film *Hotel for Dogs*, are only making it more popular, even in cities. Among the 164 breeds recognized by the AKC, the Bernese mountain dog ranks #40, up from #63 just ten years ago. It's more popular than bloodhounds, St. Bernards, border collies, greyhounds, and Irish setters. More popular than dalmations, for God's sake.

More than five years too late, I take the "Compatibility Profiler" test offered by the Bernese Mountain Dog Club of America. Typically, it starts, "Are you right for the Bernese Mountain Dog?" As I've pointed out, acquiring a purebred has more in common with applying to the Trinity School than shopping at Target.

It is a lifetime commitment, even if that lifetime is not often very long.

Here are some of the questions and my answers:

Q. I can accept a dog that lives only 7 or 8 years (no)

Q. I will willingly relax my housekeeping standards (yes)

Q. I want a dog that will have to be with the family most of the time (maybe)

Q. I live in a house with a yard (no)

Q. I live in an area with cool summers and cold, snowy winters (yes)

Q. I do not have any children (yes)

Q. I will take our dog to training classes and pursue obedience, carting (maybe)

Q. I can accept a higher risk for health problems (no)

Q. I want a dog that is self-confident, alert and good-natured but can be aloof with strangers (aloof?)

Q. My dog will be left alone regularly for more than 6 hours (yes)

The profiler's verdict is not encouraging: "Certain of your responses indicate that a Bernese Mountain Dog is not suitable for you."

Now you tell me.

The first Bernese mountain dog organization was established in 1907 in the canton of Bern, Switzerland, with seventeen members and about thirty dogs. These were very much working farm animals: milk and cheese cart pullers, watchdogs, and cattle drovers. A picture of one of the first dogs registered, Belline, shows marked points of difference from today's standard: a lower, sloping head; a wider muzzle; a higher-sitting and skinnier torso; and a noticeably flatter coat. He looks more like a rottweiler than a modern Berner.

In the 1930s, a wealthy American named Mrs. L. Egg-Leach moved to Switzerland and was struck by a dog she thought was a tricolor collie pulling a milk cart. She introduced the breed to Americans in her 1935 article, "The Bernese Is a Loyal Dog of the Swiss Alps," published in the *AKC Gazette*. In it, she echoes many Berner owners in recalling her first real-world sighting: "I think I lost my head at the time."

A few years later, the Bernese mountain dog was recognized by the AKC.

To correct a drift toward shyness and occasional aggression, a Swiss breeder in the 1940s decided to cross a Berner with a purebred Newfoundland. Newfies are truly gentle giants, beloved by Byron and Emily Dickinson. The result was a thicker-coated, sweet-natured dog, the legendary Alex v Angstorf. He was an international champion, sire of fifty-one litters, and almost all Berners in the United States today are descended from him or his sister.

Still, by the early 1970s, there were only a few hundred registered dogs in the United States. It wasn't until the 1990s that their popularity really climbed a mountain.

One nineteenth-century Swiss assessment of the breed shows that Hola is probably not all that different from her European ancestors: "They are rural in character and generally do not possess fine manners by themselves. From this it does not necessarily follow that they cannot be trained during their youth, as other dogs. But being obedient is often forgotten."

BECAUSE IT IS A WIDE-OPEN SPACE, our building's lobby has been the site of some of Hola's ripest antics. Past the doorman station, which holds Hola's favorite people on earth—namely, doormen—there are three steps down into a large marble lobby, three steps to a doggie paradise of rolling 360s, wild barking, nails slipping on rock.

In the past.

Now I make her wait at the top of the steps as I go down.

"Okay." I release.

Her eyes glimmer with recent memories of spectacular demolition derbies, drawing crowds, Bernese gone wild . . . until my *"Grrr!"* reminds her of something . . . something important . . . she's thinking as we walk . . .

By the time she remembers to misbehave, she's already doing automatic sits around the lobby perimeter.

It is during one of these automatic-sit sessions that I get a call from my friend Lilian, one of the best-known breeders of Bernese mountain dogs in the country. I'd met her at Responsible Dog Ownership Day in Madison Square Park, where she had a booth promoting the Bernese Mountain Dog Club of America, and we got to talking about her website.

"It's terrible," she'd said, one of her champion Berners standing calmly at her side. "I just learned e-mail as a senior citizen. It's a big problem for me."

I mentioned that, gosh, I happened to work in the Internet business myself, and I'd be happy to lift a mouse finger for the glorious cause, an offer she rapidly accepted.

For her site, I conducted an interview with her about her kennel and posted pictures of her litters and stud dogs. Lilian was the real deal: her kennel dominated the Bernese breed rings in the 1990s; her daughter had handled the best-in-show winners at Westminster two years in a row. (They were not Bernese mountain dogs, although one was the famous Newfoundland Josh.) Although semiretired, Lilian remained a grand lady in the breed.

A native Swiss, she has exactly the same friendly, warming presence I associate with her dogs.

"I wonder if you can do me a favor," she asks in her slightly accented English.

"Okay."

"Have you heard of Meet the Breeds?"

"Yes."

And who hasn't—posters for it are up all over Manhattan. It is AKC's blowout event at the Jacob Javits Center, where every one of the 161 recognized breeds would be present, along with every breed of cat. Because there is also going to be a CGC demonstration, I have already bought a ticket.

"I'm doing the Berner booth," she says. "And I was wondering if you could bring Hola."

"What?"

"My dogs might need a break; it's two long days, Saturday and Sunday. Can Hola come and help out?"

"You want *Hola* to represent the breed?"

"Yes, dear."

"At the biggest event of the year?"

"Yes."

"*My* Hola?"

"Why not? She's a wonderful dog. Do you think she can't do it?"

To be fair, Lilian met the actual Hola at the park, so she knows she is not a show-quality animal. I look down at my bête noire, holding her sit on my left side quite beautifully and looking up at me, beseeching me for a cookie, a crumb, a mere molecule of food. Her eyes blink and glisten. Can you spell *manipulative?*

"Of course," I lie. "We'd be honored to go. Thanks for asking."

Only a few seconds after we hang up, I am already regretting what I said.

When we get home, I call Gloria and tell her the good news. Three times. It is difficult for her to understand why anyone would want our dog to represent anything other than a cautionary tale.

"Are you sure she had the right number?" she asks.

"Be supportive," I say. "This is Hola's big break."

"She gets very stressed out. How many people are going to be there? Did Lilian tell you?"

"There could be agents," I say. "Movie people. Broadway produ—"

"You're not being fair to her. Think about the dog, Marty. She's not a show dog."

"I believe in her."

Gloria exhales on the line, as though trying to cool down her phone.

"You will be nervous," she says. "Hola will pick up on that."

"I'm meditating."

I wait for a moment before saying what I'd really called to say:

"Do you want to come with us?"

CHAPTER TWENTY-SIX

The Pickup

I DECIDE WHAT the situation calls for is an immediate run-through of the Bernese readiness situation. I have to see if my citizen canine is prepared for public consumption.

Dogs, unlike people, are extraordinarily site specific: where they are is *who* they are. So seeing my double-coated darling-in-training on the wall of my brain in a stadium with a thousand people in a crush, hands extended like cattle prods to pet her, dogs all around her, *hot* dogs all around her . . . not to mention myself, the weak strand of hemp in the rope, exuding a profound lack of faith in her manners . . . well, none of this contributes to our canine-human equanimity.

So I run her through the CGC from beginning to end, for the very first time, in the lobby of my building. Our doorman Jesus functions as the "friendly stranger" because he has a bulldog, adores Hola, and knows how to act around dogs.

And I am happy to see Hola handle test items #1 to 3 very well: she sits as Jesus approaches me and shakes my hand, stands gently as he pets her, and is, of course, so perpetually gorgeous that "Appearance and grooming" (item #3) might as well have been written by her.

We punt the crowd scenes, items #4 and 5, making do with a guy who walks by with a mouse amp and a little girl.

And like most dogs who have taken puppy kindergarten five

times, Hola's sit, down, stay, and recall are well-rehearsed and basically solid.

We skip "Reaction to another dog" (#8) because no other dogs happen by.

And her distraction resistance (#9) has been chiseled to an iron point over a half-decade trotting the sidewalks of Washington Heights.

Which leads us to the easy #10, "Supervised separation," where the dog is left with an unknown person for three minutes while the owner goes out of sight. I have always assumed this item is so easy that not only have we never trained for it—what's to train?—but we have never even tried it.

"Never mind the last one," I say to Jesus, "you probably have to get back to the desk."

"Let's do it," he says. "My Bo had big trouble with it."

"Why?"

"You'll see."

And I do.

I say, as we are instructed to do, "Will you watch my dog, please?" Then I surrender the leash to Jesus and walk away.

The requirement to pass this item is simple: the dog must *not* show signs of agitation, including, as enumerated in the evaluators' guidelines: whining, howling, barking, pacing, panting, breathing hard, pulling, acting insecure, or eliminating on the evaluator's shoe.

No sooner had I turned my back to leave than Hola starts in on the first one.

I go into the mailbox area, closing the door behind me, and I can hear her whining get more and more frantic. At thirty seconds, she has graduated to full-throated barks.

"*Stay, girl! Stay there!*" from Jesus is replaced, within a few seconds, by: "*Calm the fuck down Hola!*"

And her feet scratching on the marble floor and—

At forty-five seconds I swing open the door, and Hola rips herself away from Jesus and runs toward me as though I've just returned from ten years at sea.

"Well," says Jesus with a certain unattractive wisdom, "that one needs a little work."

And then my phone rings.

I MEET MY FRIEND DARRYL, the soft-spoken lawyer, in the lobby of a new twenty-story condo on West Sixty-third Street, just east of the Lincoln Center–Fordham University complex.

The super standing next to him is pint-sized and flat-faced, black-haired, with a hard conspiratorial mouth, and as I come in off the street and shake out my umbrella from the rain, I see him and Darryl huddled over the house phone on the front desk, staring at it as though it is about to move.

"What's going on?" I ask them.

The two older men turn to me with deeply tired eyes, and I realize this "situation"—as Darryl had described it to me on the phone—is a lot more serious than I thought.

"He's not letting anybody in," says Darryl. "Not answering the door."

"His voice mail is full," I say.

"This gentleman is going to let us in. We might have to take him . . . take him to—"

"He has a sister, right?"

"We called her," says the super, whose name I never got, "but she's tired of his bullshit."

"Hold on," I say. "He's done this before?"

"Like twenty times. Can't say I blame her at all. It's horrible to say but—"

"Let's just go upstairs," says Darryl.

The whole way down in the cab I was obsessing about item #10. I could not believe we'd come so far, worked so hard, and that we still wouldn't get our CGC because Hola had decided to make another item the one she just won't do.

I'd succeeded in getting her to stop jumping on people, in controlled situations, and then the exercise I take for granted becomes the one she will almost definitely fail. Why that one? The *easiest* one? The one I then believed, wrongly, cannot even be trained.

It felt to me as though Hola was trying to mock me, trick me, yes, stab me in the back.

Dogs under stress will practice displacement, doing something like sniffing the ground furiously when you're trying to train them to retrieve; it's how they wish something away. Looking back, I was performing my own human displacement to avoid dealing with what Darryl had told me on the phone.

And, really, it isn't until we follow the little super into the eighth-floor studio apartment and see what is in there that I let go of the CGC. For what we enter is a nightmare, one that in many ways still hasn't stopped.

The hallway is very dark, although it is daytime. There is a mildly antiseptic smell in the air, like lemon-scented Lysol. We step over an arsenal of corrugated Grey Goose vodka cartons, and the super turns on the light in the hallway.

I remember the stunning silence, the scream of lowered shades.

Darryl forges down the hallway into the living room, repeating, "Clark? Are you here? It's Darryl and Marty. The super let us in. Clark? Are you decent? Clark?"

He has a deep and calm voice, and a surplus of what Cesar would call calm-assertive energy. Usually dressed in country-squire casual from Orvis, he is a tall man with militaristic hair that he treats with floral-scented oils, strident blue eyes, a weak-ish nose, and a sharp chin he conceals behind some carefully pruned steel-gray foliage.

One of the top criminal attorneys in the city at one point, he is now retired to a duplex on West End Avenue with a third or fourth partner, a man he obviously adores, and a six-year-old adopted son with some developmental issues. He is about seventy, has ten years' sobriety, and sponsors a lot of women and a few straight men, including Clark.

As the super goes into the kitchen flipping on lights, I follow Darryl into the living room.

Décor is Ikea modern but surprisingly sparse. A yellow-gold carpet covers the floor, and the furniture consists of a dark-brown leather sofa, a cheap halogen floor lamp, and the world's largest HD television set bolted to the wall. I don't see a book, a table, a picture, a pet.

I don't see a life.

But then, stepping around the front of the sofa, I spot the distinctive navy-blue paperback cover of the Big Book lying on the carpet. On top of it, squared in its center like a design exercise, is the iPhone Clark has stopped answering.

In a way, the absence of clutter—things like pizza boxes, candy bar wrappers, crushed beer cans, cigarette butts—is much more alarming than a big pile of crap. It betrays a state of mind at a very odd angle from life.

"Not here," says Darryl. "Are you sure he didn't leave?"

"Sure, I'm sure," says the super. "I watched him stumble up this morning, and I've been on all day."

"There another way out?"

"Nope. Gotta go past me."

"Then he's in the bedroom," I say.

Darryl and I look at one another and simultaneously think: *After you.*

I see now that this is a small apartment, maybe eight hundred square feet in total, much smaller than I'd imagined a successful banker with a large, rambunctious family would enjoy. I see no evidence that there had ever been a boxer named Joey living here, and, believe me, there would be evidence. The kitchen looks like a white box with a stove. The living room like a movie theater in the middle of the night.

And the bedroom—well, the bedroom is an absolute wreck.

The door to the bedroom is at the end of a short, windowless corridor. Darryl, being bolder than I am, leads the way. He flips the light switch, but nothing happens.

"Bulb burned out," he says, needlessly. Then he knocks on the door, says, "Hey, Clark, you in there?"

And we go in.

Light-blocking shades are drawn, which makes the odor more prominent. Vomit, layered with the sickly twinge of something that smells like cough syrup.

"Clark?"

I step carefully to the window and open the shades. I see the walls first: they've been sprayed with a layer of bile, laced with blood, as though from an airbrush, but it happened days ago now because the residue is dried and flaking off the paint. The only furniture is a king-size bed whose sheets have been stripped and lie in a pile on the floor at its foot.

A thin pad of broken glass shards surrounds the bed as though they are tiles waiting to be set. A pile of a dozen or so vodka bottles rises from the glass-mined carpet under the rain-spattered window like an offering to some pagan god of the hunt.

"Shit," says Darryl. "Wow."

"I'm sorry," says the super. "We should've done this sooner. I thought he wanted . . ."

Then, as one, we pivot to the bathroom-door handle, which is turning, moving downward, and the door eases open and there is Clark the Banker looking like a hundred square miles of graveyard in a storm.

His habitual red rugby shirt is untucked and caked with mucous and spit, and his rumpled tan khakis sit low on his hips. He isn't wearing his glasses and his eyes are cavernous and black, shot through with bloody spiders, and his skin is damp, pale, and loose. His hair, strangely, is wet; moisture drips onto his shoulders as he sways in place, staring not at us but at a point among us, below us, into a reality that is deeper than our own.

"Hey guysh," he slurs, with a slippery smile, "hey there."

"How you doing?" I ask him.

"Fuck you," he says and falls forward.

After the EMTs gurney an unconscious Clark into the Roosevelt Hospital Emergency Room, Darryl and I sit for ten hours in the waiting area unable to learn much of anything, except that he is still alive.

I don't know Darryl all that well, but those hours together bring us closer, and he tells me some of what I'd been unable to see for myself.

"I think Clark's been drinking on and off for years," Darryl says.

"He told me he had like ten years' sober."

"We are liars. You should know that."

"What about his family? His wife?"

"He's been divorced since I knew him, four or five years. There's kids but he lost custody because of the drinking. He hasn't seen them in at least that long. Doesn't talk to his wife."

"I can't believe it," I say. "He told me—what about his job? He should go to rehab, right? Can he take time off?"

Darryl looks at me with a kind of terrible pity.

"Oh, Marty," he says to me, shaking his head, "he hasn't worked in years. The guy lost everything. He doesn't have anything left."

"That dog? Was he a lie too?"

"What dog?"

"Joey the boxer."

All Darryl does is shrug, and the badly dressed crowd suffers around us in the pain of mandatory bad news pounding them from the TVs mounted in the corners of the room.

"Oh my God," I say suddenly, touching Darryl's vivid orange Thomas Pink shirtsleeve. "I just realized something."

"What?"

"Why Clark gave me that cat of his, Ruby."

"Why?"

"Because he knew he couldn't take care of her. He loved the cat."

Around hour eight, when we are both beginning to wonder how much we really want to suffer for this guy Clark anyway, Darryl breaks a pensive silence: "It was the God Thing."

We say it like that, capital letters: the God Thing. All of us know what it means. We're in a spiritual program, a God-centered program, and a lot of people at first really wish that it weren't.

"Oh, yeah?"

"How are you with that?"

"Okay," I say. "I believe in God. More or less."

"It sends more people out than anything else. It's too bad. Clark kept saying, 'I know I'm an alcoholic, but I'm just not comfortable with the God Thing.' And I'm nodding my sympathy nod, you know, 'Yes, I understand, of course; why would you be?' "

"Right."

"But I'm saying, 'So you think you're the fucking center of the universe? There's nothing more powerful than you are? Can you think of anything?' He was saying, 'No, I really can't.' And I start listing things like the government, the national parks, Yosemite, Alzheimer's, earthquakes, the rain—"

"Harvard Business School—"

"You know, death. Death is bigger than you are."

We stop talking for a while, both of us thinking that within a year Clark the Ex-Banker could quite plausibly be dead.

The next day I take Hola to church. It happens to be the annual Feast of St. Francis, the day on which good Catholic animals like Hola are blessed, so we drive down to my parish at the Church of St. Paul the Apostle near Lincoln Center.

"I'm going to need you to be properly receptive to the Holy Spirit," I tell her. "Open your heart and pray for God's blessing."

What's a Holy Spirit? she asks, her eyes narrowing skeptically in the rearview mirror.

"It's complicated," I say. "It's like a feeling you get."

Like when you and Mom are together?

"Don't go there."

That's my favorite time, she seems to say. *I love that.*

"I know, honey."

When's she coming back?

"Can I get an Our Father and a couple Hail Marys, please?"

Our church looks like a Romanesque cathedral and was built in the late nineteenth century. It has a cavernous rectangular interior like a hangar for a blessed blimp, a Stanford White altar in the back with carved stone idols, and an ornate wooden shelf of pipes that slit open and closed as the Gothic organ sings. Apses and side altars are filigreed and baroque, and the overall effect of the space always feels to me like being in an empty football field at the beginning of the day at the tail end of winter.

Even when it's filled, it's full of open space. It has a thriving congregation of tourists and regulars, and the 10 a.m. Mass with the choir is the highlight of my week. The most beautiful cantors on earth sing like sun falling on a mountain.

Amid a din of barking and yowls, Father Gil leads us all through the St. Francis Prayer and a brief poetic homily:

"We bless these animals who have brought so much joy to
our lives.
They give entirely of themselves and contribute to our
spiritual selves.
They are the flesh of our flesh, joined to us in love.
That as Francis knew was a mirror or reflection of God's
love for us.
For it is all the same love.
And it wells up in us, makes us whole, and cleanses us."

Normally, Father Gil is not drawn to heightened language. His homilies tend to be brief, deeply felt, and pragmatic. Taking notes is not required.

But the yelps and the meows, the woman holding up the ashes of her dead dog, so rawly that I feel like they're still warm from the fire, and the absurdity of a stuffed-animal family being held aloft for blessing by a kid barely old enough to think —all this inspires him.

Then he comes around with the wet scepter and sprinkles the pets. Pushing through the crowd, getting each one with a generous aim.

He kisses the urn.

"Well," he says coming up to Hola. "That's a big boy there."

"She's a girl, Father."

"What a beauty."

"Thank you, Father," I say. "She's new to the faith."

"Good for her."

Hola gets a double dose of holy water.

She stands still for a moment, puzzled, as though she's about to remember that she hates water but doesn't.

Hola prays before her blessing.

CHAPTER TWENTY-SEVEN

Meet the Breeds

THE DAY BEFORE the Meet the Breeds event, I decide the best way to prepare Hola is to wear her out physically so she'll be too tired to do anything in the chaos but sit quietly for petting.

That's my theory, anyway.

Even on our best days together, when I imagine I see progress, I still feel like Susan Conant's Holly Winter, who said of one of her malamutes that he "doesn't necessarily do anything more than take my opinions under advisement."

So I saddle her up and walk her north to the New York– Presbyterian Hospital campus, around the Neurological Institute, where clearly I should have been a patient, past all the alarmingly young future health care providers in their day-old scrubs.

And on the way back I'm refreshing our dominance training when I hear a little *snap!*

She looks startled a moment, then she's fine, sniffing the mounds of garbage we laughingly call a sidewalk on 159th Street.

But she's limping.

Her right front paw can barely hold any of her weight at all, like when she gets salt in one of her paws in the winter—which happens all the time in Manhattan—and she cannot put any pressure on it until I extract the crystals from between her toes.

I check but can't see anything stuck in her foot. We limp home and I disinfect the paw, but there is no visible contusion, lesion, puncture, or rash.

Leaving me to face the fact: I broke my dog's foot.

She doesn't get to go to Meet the Breeds—and it isn't even her fault.

Ruby cuts into the sound of my blood coming to a gel by hopping onto the doggie bed cushion next to Hola and kneading it with her paws like a miniature pastry chef wearing little white gloves.

While I am waiting in Midtown at the doggie ER for the vet to return with the verdict, I call Gloria to tell her she doesn't need to come in for the big dog show after all.

"You're working her too hard," she says. "Why are you doing this to her?"

"It's not that serious."

"You broke the dog's paw, Marty. That's serious."

"We don't know if it's—"

"I'm getting an idea what your childhood was like."

"What?"

"It's a pretty dark world," she says. "You're pushing her to get this stupid certificate, but it doesn't mean anything. It's not good for her; it's not good for you. You're not listening to her. She'll do anything to make you happy, you know, she'll . . . she'll . . ."

"Are you crying? Don't cry, Gloria. Come on." I am pleading now, feeling like I've done something even more terrible than the terrible thing I have, in fact, done.

She sniffs a couple times, blows her nose over the line.

"Look," she says, "be careful with Hola. Okay?"

"I promise. I love Hola."

"I know you do."

"I'm sorry, hon."

"I know."

The ER vet tells me that her paw is not broken, just sprained, and that there isn't really anything I can do for her.

"Just take it easy," she says. "Let her rest."

"I know," I say. "One day at a time."

Meet the Breeds is held in the Jacob Javits Center, a convention behemoth beside the Hudson River on the far West Side of Manhattan, just south of Midtown. A concrete monolith that seems like nothing so much as a monument to the Mob. There are clotted lines for tickets and coat check, and people are not allowed to bring their own dogs, an inspired idea. Inside are booths pushing pet food and dog jewelry, portable crates and obedience clubs. And there is a show ring the size of a baseball infield surrounded by risers and folding chairs four or five rows deep for the major demonstrations—agility, carting, police dogs, flyball, and obedience.

At the back wall there are more than one hundred live displays devoted to almost every breed the AKC recognizes, placed in alphabetical order. I imagine the logistical nightmare involved—some of these breeds are almost comically rare. Yes, there are Labs and Yorkies and shepherds, but there are also xolos and pharaoh hounds. Some of the reps I talk to drove all the way from the West Coast to be here. Almost every breed of dog is included, except, it turns out, the golden retriever, whose booth sits oddly dark.

The forty or so cat breeds are sequestered in a smaller bull pen to the north. Their area is entirely less energetic and popular. Most dog people agree with Holly Winter: "*Dog* spelled backward? Yes. But *cat*? Tac? I didn't see the cosmic significance."

I would feel sorry for the cats except that, when I visit them later in the day, out of pity, they seem absolutely overwhelmed by indifference. Most of them, in fact, are asleep. I get the impression they find this event altogether too people pleasing for their taste.

Which is why we love cats.

In addition to stopping by my friend Lilian's Bernese mountain dog booth, I am hoping to get a consultation with the well-known animal behaviorist, operant-conditioning expert, and author Mary Burch. She is the head of the AKC's Canine Good Citizen program and its official public face: I'd seen a clip of her on the *Today* show talking about how, well, every dog can be one.

In other words, lying.

She seemed like a gracious southern woman, and I knew she was about to publish a book called *Citizen Canine,* the first comprehensive guide to the CGC program since Jack and Wendy Volhard's ten-year-old effort.

I locate her giving the test as a demo in a small ring placed awkwardly in the middle of a walkway among the vendor booths, pushed up against a concession stand dispensing giant pretzels.

There is a line of people waiting to be tested. Mary is a commanding, stylish woman with a clipboard. Rather more made-up, highlighted, perm-waved, and basically more put together than your typical dog woman, who seems to think high fashion is anything without a urine stain.

The dogs are suspiciously adept—sailing through the requirements. One woman pops out a treat and is immediately expelled. But other than that, the canine manners on display are excellent. My spirits sink faster than a mastiff in a mudslide until I discover the reason: these are all trained demo dogs. They already have their CGC.

After watching awhile, I leave and push my way through the crowd to the Bernese mountain dog display. It is decorated with a Swiss flag and some prints of generic Alpine scenes. A small space for such big dogs, with two crates and a pen, each of which holds a grinning, calm Berner. A couple of Lilian's friends are here, including a skinny guy with a perm whose dog is attached to a traditional Swiss milk cart.

Throngs of people pressing in, crowding. Their arms out. Asking if these dogs shed a lot, how long they live, whether they are particularly well-behaved.

Now, if these are your criteria, I can save you a trip to the kennel: don't get a Bernese mountain dog. They shed all the time, so much so that dog hair will eventually become a quilt on top of your furniture. They live maybe eight or nine years, if you're lucky. And if you've been paying attention, you'll know exactly what they're like to train.

But, yowza, are they popular.

"Is Hola feeling any better?" Lilian asks me.

"She's resting."

"Can you bring her tomorrow?"

Visions of Hola hopping onto old ladies and jabbing at them lovingly with her good front paw. A scream rings out. A stampede of spooked, snarling purebreds.

"Well," I say, "I'm not sure about her paw."

Something about Lilian—so open-faced, such a bringer of four-legged life—I didn't want to mislead her, not exactly.

"She gets very anxious," I add in the understatement of the month.

Lilian's friend Debbie, who I like immediately, hears something in my voice and performs a rescue operation:

"Don't worry about it," she says. "Listen to the dog."

. . .

By the time I get back to the CGC mini-ring, the demos are over. I spend some time wandering around, and, as so often happens, it is at the moment when I've given up on casually running into Mary Burch that I do, in fact, casually run into her.

On my way out the door, I take a brief stop at a table of dog-training books from the BowTie Press. And when I look up, there she is, standing beside me.

So I introduce myself and say, "I was watching your demonstration earlier."

"Oh, yes." As in: *You're the freak who was stalking my ring.*

"I wanted to say hi," I say.

"Hi." And *buh bye.*

She throws me a bone: "Are you enjoying the event today?"

"It's very successful," I say. "I was over at the Bernese mountain dog booth this afternoon; there were hundreds of people. I have a Berner myself."

She smiles. "That's what Berners do to people."

"We're trying to get the CGC. It's been very hard for us."

"Why?"

"Mostly it's item ten, 'Supervised separation.' We're struggling with—"

"How are you training it?"

"You can train it?" I say. "I thought—"

"Of course you can. Here's what you do. You should—"

Just then, some asshole wearing a black BowTie Press baseball cap leans over the book table and says, "Mary, you have a second?"

"Excuse me," she says, turning away from me just as I'm about to learn the secret.

. . .

I LOOK OVER at the main obedience ring and see a lanky black Lab being led in by a beautiful, athletic woman with radioactive highlights and a fake-baked face that is as serious as an astronaut's. Without quite realizing it, I'm drawn physically to ringside in time to witness something I will never forget all the days of my life.

"Welcome," booms the PA, "Petra Ford and Tyler. They were the winners of the National Obedience Invitational last year and are going to Long Beach next month to defend their title."

Later, I find out that Petra is the Cindy Crawford of dog trainers, a former competitive cyclist who has handled her incredible Lab Tyler to the very top ranks of competitive canine obedience. Her upper body is remarkably still, and she has no expression at all as she touches her left hand to her abdomen and says something inaudible, bringing Tyler into perfect heel position at her side.

The emcee explains that in March, Petra and Tyler will be going to compete with the U.S. team at the canine world championships at Crufts in England.

"That's why Petra is not smiling," says the emcee. "Any kind of expression can be considered a double cue in the English system—a facial expression on top of a hand signal could be giving the dog two different ways to get what the handler wants. Only one cue's allowed."

Petra and Tyler proceed to pace through the English practice of heeling patterns at three different speeds—superslow, normal, and fast.

What am I seeing: a simple heeling pattern. Tyler trots off leash next to Petra with his head slightly in front of her left knee, his eyes watching her face—purely the grace of the body, a tension of moving and forgetting, because at Crufts you can't say a word to your dog during the entire five-minute heeling pattern: only hand cues are allowed.

The judge whispers instructions to Petra, who leads Tyler through the figures: "Left, right, halt, about, circle left, halt, straight."

The ideal impression should be that the dog is attached to the handler by a magnet. An invisible line. Which, in a way, he is. The dog is so eager, yet calm, with no reinforcement at all. Doing what it has been trained to do, for years now. Just as athletic as Petra, just as focused on her as she is on him.

It will tell you something about how seriously I am taking this unbelievable showcase of human-canine teamwork that when they are done I wonder why it is my new glasses are so terrible and I realize that my eyes are filling up with tears.

CHAPTER TWENTY-EIGHT

Petra Ford

SHORTLY AFTER Meet the Breeds, Petra Ford became the two-time winner of the AKC's most prestigious competitive obedience event, the National Obedience Invitational, with her black Labrador retriever, NOC2 OTCh Count Tyler Show Me the Money UDX4 OM1, called Tyler. I spoke to her shortly after her historic second win.

"The invitational is a tough event. Day one each team does six rounds of Open and Utility,* plus the long stays. Second day it's head-to-head elimination rounds. The final two teams do full rounds of Open and Utility. So you're in the ring like twelve times over the two days. And if you make what's called a substantial—a major error—you're basically out. It's a tremendous amount of pressure on the dog and the handler.

"Mentally, it's very draining, stressful for the dog. They can totally descend to that environment. They pick up on everything; they're dogs, you know. Tyler acts different there than he does anywhere else. He's a different dog. It's hard to relax, but also the waiting and going in again—start and stop. I didn't really watch the other people. I don't watch. The second day I

---

*The AKC's two classes of obedience competition. Open requires intricate heeling patterns and retrieves and leads to the Companion Dog Excellent title (CD/CDX). Utility is more advanced and requires scent discrimination and jumps, leading to the Utility Dog title (UD/UDX).

don't talk to anybody really. We come out of the ring. I have my friend Stella there who helps me. She has Tyler's favorite toy. We give it to him as a reward, and we go out into the hallway.

"We do a lot of physical work. Before 2008, I started Tyler on the treadmill, increasing the speed and the incline. We did about twenty minutes three times a week, tapering down before the competition. This year we also did it underwater. We conditioned longer this year. I had a lot of dog—maybe too much dog.

"What I like is a happy working dog. Where I train in New Jersey, we emphasize the importance of the dog being happy. A lot of trainers will just get caught up in drilling their dog. What's the point of that, huh?"

"I got into the sport late. Didn't have any pets as a kid. My mother would not let me get a dog. I was a professional cyclist. I did all right, I guess. My mental state was terrible, very bad. I was always down on myself, feeling like I was no good, that I wasn't going to win.

"I started training for serious with my yellow Lab, Duncan. I wanted to do agility, but I went somewhere and it wasn't motivating. I found this place in the phone book and drove out there. Started taking privates with a teacher there. I just retrained Duncan from the ground up. He really started liking it. Then I got Tyler. I know he's my once-in-a-lifetime special dog.

"We keep the training interesting. Every day I have a couple things I want to accomplish. Specific goals for that day. As soon as he does them two or three times, we move on. Always end on a positive note. Every exercise is broken in little pieces. And I use rewards. When he does it right, he'll get a reward, a toy, a game. I mix up the rewards.

"The big difference came because we did a huge amount of

mental work. I used to be just in a terrible place mentally. In the ring I was always nervous, always negative, not confident at all. Just like when I was cycling. I began to realize, if I was going to ask my dog to perform at an optimum level, I had to ask the same thing of myself. So I got that book *It's Not Just About the Ribbons.** Did the exercises in that book, the visualizations. I started to visualize us doing the perfect exercise, being calm, working together. It made a huge difference. I took that very seriously.

"I have to stay very still in the ring, very calm. Tyler will feed off the energy, and if I give him anything he'll run with it. I have to stay totally focused and quiet. People can't even hear me talking to him in the ring.† But I do."

*By Jane Savoie, a horse rider and trainer whose methods of positive self-talk and visualization are widely used by competitive dog trainers.
†Talking to the dog is allowed in U.S. competitions.

CHAPTER TWENTY-NINE

The Rock House

PETRA FORD OPENS A DOOR in my heart: she shows me that dog training is a form of art and an act of love. I've never seen two beings listen so carefully to each other or care so much. I think of Gloria. I think of Hola.

Humility is not thinking less of myself. It is thinking of myself less.

Then I call the AKC and try to set up a real interview with Mary Burch. What I want is some inside help with item #10. Needless to say, the AKC, being practiced operant conditioners, do what trainers do when confronted with a behavior they want to go away: they ignore me. As Lorena said, ignoring attention seeking is the highest form of dominance.

As the silence from the organization whose slogan is "We're more than champion dogs, we're the dog's champion" all but bites me in the leg, I focus on getting more of what trainers call "persistence, frequency, and duration" from my dog. At night, after our walk, I have her do sit-stays in front of our building. I choose a spot with maximum traffic, where we can test her ability to maintain the stay. Even when there is actual canine-human eye contact and—her aphrodisiac—a smile.

One night, a Friday, I am drilling her in the lobby as a stream of my neighbors surges past, returning from work.

"Hello," I say. "Hello, hello."

"She's doing well," they say. "Much better. Keep it up."

"Thanks."

"Can I pet her?" ask others, the ones who don't know her well.

"We're working on her manners."

"Oh."

Our doorman Jesus is standing at a respectful distance, sideways, like a real dog person, using a calming posture.

"Looks like she's doing better," he says, watching her sit. "Getting more consistent with the attention. You been working her a lot."

"She's a good girl," I say.

"You should show Gloria."

"She's not around."

"I know," he says. Of course he knows; doormen in Manhattan co-ops know more than the tenants do about their lives. "You should show her. She'd be real impressed. We miss her around here."

"Uh-huh," I say. "Uh-huh."

So the next morning, we rent yet another car and drive two hours west to the Rock House, and I don't call ahead or alert the media, which for the entire duration of the drive, I am pretty sure is a stupid thing to do.

I can't call my friend Clark, who is in a twenty-eight-day detox unit upstate, so I jingle his sponsor, Darryl, who is reliably more romantic than sensible.

"You're surprising Gloria with a drive-by?" he says. "That's actually kind of sweet."

"Are you sure? Do you think she'll think I'm checking up on her?"

"Hey, she's your wife, right? You Catholics are married for life."

"She's not Catholic."

"Pray for her."

Some people call around to get the advice they've already given themselves. I don't have to bother. I get it first time out.

Winter falls earlier in the high Catskills, which always seems to be about twenty degrees cooler and two centuries older than the city.

Vegetation thins as we plunge into Sullivan County, and, as if from a spring toy, billboards appear for well drillers, ambulance chasers, and the casinos and racetrack of Monticello. It's a region that hasn't been prosperous in half a century, since air-conditioning and affordable air travel to Florida destroyed the need for a nearby summer vacation place for the tristate middle class. It's been reduced to a string of derelict towns and abandoned campgrounds that are rented by ultraorthodox Jews, the kind too strict to make eye contact with me.

Still, it's very restful up there, maybe because nobody has any money and all the yards, and children, need a little work. Abandoned, empty shells of farmhouses push up against the road, on which every second vehicle is an eighteen-wheeler hauling a crane, a backhoe, or raw lumber for a building site.

I stop at the Mobil station at the intersection near our house, across from the decrepit motor lodge with the rusting wrecked cars, sitting like forgotten sculptures from some 1960s conceptual art show, in its weed-choked parking lot.

"Wait here, Hola," I say, as I always do. "I'll be right back."

You got it, she seems to say. *I'm in the zone.*

She's been a good girl all the way up, not whining much since we crossed the G. W. Bridge, sleeping through most of New Jersey, later lustily eyeing the open fields and BBQ stands along the desolate expanse of Route 17B past the trotting track.

The guy behind the register at the Mobil Mini-Mart is an old, bow-legged Pakistani named Prahad. I know him well from all the summer weekends I've spent out here over the years.

"Long time," he says, ringing up my seltzer and Slim Jim.

"Yup."

"Your wife is here. Came in a while ago."

"How is she?"

He eyes me curiously; it is, I suppose, a puzzling question to come from a husband.

"Good," he says. "Pretty happy."

This is not music to my ears.

"Hola," I say, as we drive the twisting half mile past the ice-cream-and-chicken stand to the house, "what if Mommy doesn't want to see us."

She'll want to see me, she says. *Everybody loves me.*

"Don't count on it, girlfriend."

Do you think she made crab cakes?

The Rock House sits on a massive boulder, the result of glacial runoff millennia ago, amid a thin forest of trees grown to extraordinary height to capture rare fingers of light. During any of the frequent rainstorms in the area, one of these trees often splits with a crack and topples, leaving us with a strange prehistoric backyard of dense rotting tree trunks and fungi that never see sun.

As Hola and I pull up the hill to the house, I see our blue Echo parked near the front door.

Fallen leaves are piled up on the hill next to the little shed and around the house, as though someone got tired of raking them up. I stop the car and study the house: the same white trim around a bright red door, the new shingled roof that never leaks, a polite stream of smoke coming out of the fireplace indicating the lady of the house is home.

"This was a mistake," I say to Hola. "We should have called first."

Well, she says, *we're here now. We own this place. Let's go have some lunch.*

"Gloria's gonna be mad."

Maybe she cooked something nice. She's an excellent chef. Chicken?

I open the back door of the rental car and let Hola out, snapping on her harness, just as Gloria emerges through the red door.

CHAPTER THIRTY

Mary Burch

"WELL, HELLO," she says, without obvious signs of annoyance. "I didn't know you two were coming."

I look at her. She is more beautiful than I have been dreaming: well rested, calm, slim but not gaunt like she gets in the city, wearing her tan riding pants and a blue hunter vest buttoned neatly to her neck, her hair tied back in a pony tail. She looks wary, perhaps, but not clearly angry, holding her riding hat under her arm.

Now, we go into action.

"Okay, Hola," I say. "Let's show Gloria what we can do. Sit."

I can see Hola's mind moving: she wants badly to run to her mommy, but she hesitates long enough for me to *grrr* and snap the leash.

She sits, and I have her attention.

"Good girl," I say.

I give her the signal to stay, flat palm down in front of her nose. Leaving Hola, I walk up to Gloria and say, "Hello."

Watching the dog carefully, she takes my hand and shakes it.

"Hello," she says. "What are you doing?"

"Watch this."

I go back to Hola as calmly as I can and say her release word: *Okay.*

She stands, her head shifting rapidly back and forth between my face and Gloria's. I need to keep her focused here.

"Heel," I say, tucking my left arm at my side and walking straight ahead.

She follows me, looking up to see if I have anything for her.

"No treats," I whisper. "Heel."

We do a right turn, an about-turn, a left, and then I stop.

I say nothing.

She sits—the automatic sit so beloved of obedience types. Every time the handler stops, the dog sits without being asked, without a signal.

"Down," I say, lifting my hand out in front of her, and she drops.

"Stay," with the signal. I walk ten yards, twenty yards, without looking back. I know Gloria is thinking the same thing I am at that moment: there is a road at the end of our driveway, and nothing between Hola and it but her training.

I am not afraid, though; I feel in my heart she will stay, and she does.

"Hola, come," I say, and she runs toward me, finishing with a sit in front of me, looking up.

"Good girl," I say. "Okay."

She stands and I grab the leash, praising her lavishly, and put her into a heel for our trip back to Gloria. I let Gloria pet her for a minute—a touching mother and child reunion.

"I see you two have been busy," Gloria says. "I'm impressed."

"She's doing good."

"You two look great, "she says. "Healthy."

"Thanks."

"I'm late for my riding lesson. I have to go. Sorry."

"That's okay."

She looks at me, expectantly, and I think she is going to tell me something.

"Can you move the car?" she says. "I can't back out."

Hola sleeps most of the way back to the city, until we get to the bridge to Manhattan, when she starts whining.

I say, "I know how you feel, girl. I know exactly how you feel."

WHEN WE GET BACK HOME there is an e-mail message from the AKC saying that Mary Burch will talk to me. When I get her on the phone, it turns out she's a genetically warm woman with a deep-fried southern accent and an acidic sense of humor.

I tell her I enjoyed Meet the Breeds very much.

"It was better than the typical dog show," she says, "because you're not just preaching to the converted."

"Yeah, there were civilians there. Families."

"That ring where I did the demos was too small, scrunched in the middle like that. We won't do it like that again."

"The CGC is important," I say. "It should be out in the main ring."

"How's your dog doing with it?"

Here, I describe a moving narrative of our struggle with item #10.

"The mistake people make with that one," she says, "is they don't train for it. They show up at the test and expect the dog to do it without ever having practiced. Owners are confused because it doesn't look like a trained behavior in the sense of sit or down."

"It does seem like it should be easy," I say. "But Hola starts getting upset after twenty seconds."

Mary Burch breathes out dramatically, as people often do when contemplating the logic of dogs.

"Some dogs," she says, "can do separation from the day they are born. They are hang-loose dogs who are happy to hang out and wait for you to come back. For dogs who have bonded strongly with their owners, this can be a difficult item."

"Yup."

She tells me to try shaping it with a cue every time, like "Wait," and starting with a few seconds' absence, gradually increasing the duration of the separation, second by second. Which sounds fine until I remember that the specified separation period is three minutes long. That's a lot of seconds to pile on one by one.

"We have a dog at home, he's a UD"—Utility Dog, an advanced title obtained by fewer than one-tenth of one percent of dogs in the United States each year—"and I don't know if he'd pass that item. He's so attached to my husband. But he hates me. I take the leash, and he sneers at me and goes three steps away."

"Sounds like we have a preferred-parent situation."

"And how."

She talks about how the CGC evaluator wants to see "some shred of relationship between the handler and the dog," one in which the dog pays attention and the handler is fair. And we talk about items that were modified over the years, how evaluators get some leeway in the ring, and what the program is really all about.

"Every year thousands of dogs are abandoned to shelters because of behavior problems," she tells me, with obvious passion. "And these are things that can be corrected with just basic training. Dogs are being killed because of lack of training, and that's what the Canine Good Citizen program is all about."

CHAPTER THIRTY-ONE

Television

A FEW NIGHTS LATER, I am sitting on my sofa in front of the television rereading Susan Conant's latest Holly Winter book, *All Shots*, eating Oreos, and running my fingers through Hola's freshly shampooed fur: "Behind every so-called coincidence," Conant writes, "lies a series of connections, some small, some large, that, if traced back far enough, lead inevitably to the great source of meaning and purpose in this otherwise senseless universe, namely, dogs."

Ruby is kneading the sofa cushion at my head like there is a rush order for a dozen tiny pizzas.

The TV is muted, since I prefer to imagine that what is being said is more interesting than it actually is. A promo spot comes on for a show about "ordinary" people who suddenly lose their minds and do terrible things. Usually, it turns out these so-called ordinary people had a long history of drug abuse and mental illness, but, still, it's a cautionary tale. Gloria watched this show regularly; I could always tell when it was on because she would call me at work and suddenly thank me for not running a meth lab or having a secret sex slave. I am grateful to *48 Hours: Mystery* for making me look good. And I am feeling mutedly hopeful about our CGC test, scheduled for the coming weekend.

The now-silent program is Conan O'Brien's *Tonight Show*, before it gets canceled, and his guest is Gabourey Sidibe, the young star of the searing dramatic tour de force *Precious*. I hadn't seen that particular tour de force myself, since I avoid suicidally depressing films, but her silent charm makes me unmute the sound on the TV and listen up.

Gabourey says something modest and moving; Conan responds with a comment so glib it blinds the eyes; there's a trickle of laughter; and as it's dripping down, Gabourey utters a word I cannot believe I am hearing.

A single word that has convinced me to this day that we are all connected in this life, that our smallest actions—if done with conviction and in a spirit of service—can yodel through the canyons of this country like a warning from a village on the farther shore of love.

She says: "Totes."

CHAPTER THIRTY-TWO

Canine Good Citizen

. . . So WE ENTER THE RING.

Hola weighs in at a trim and angular eighty-five, a solid weight, all sinew now and deep fluffy fur. Carefully rinsed, raked, and combed out for her Canine Good Citizen test. Her coloring is glorious in the harsh interior light of the Port Chester Obedience Training Club, blasted by a winter blizzard: white paws a-trot, grounding a deep black torso and cottony chest as white as spun sugar. A streamlined muzzle with a brush of blaze driving up her nose to those determined amber eyes.

She trots into the center and I whisper, "Okay, girl. It's on!"

The ref comes toward us, wearing a gym teacher's smile, in regulation baggy jeans, pale-blue sweatshirt, and graying hair over snowy skin that hasn't seen a beach since the Summer of Love.

"Hola, sit," I say and check my fighter as she does.

She takes the measure of the ring, a girl who only really comes alive on stage. Classmates from her Family Manners and CGC prep classes taken over the past few months dot the side walls in pained anticipation:

Alex, the black Lab who can do almost nothing, and little Brewster, the poodle who loves Hola so much he lies down sometimes and just watches her breathe. There's Cody, the unspayed German shepherd bitch who's the world's scariest-looking cupcake, and like many of the others is trying for her Therapy Dog certification today. And Bob, the Havanese who is a genius and a gymnast, teacher's pet and egomaniac, a legend in his own two-ounce mind.

Hola scans them, eye to eye, as she sits by my left leg, nodding slightly, acknowledging their support and encouragement during the long, wintry months of struggle she has totally forgotten.

I scan the onlookers myself to see if Gloria is there, but I know she can't be. The roads are almost closed. Driving down here in this storm would be too dangerous.

It's a large ring, maybe a thousand square feet, well lighted, with a computer-screen-blue pad underfoot and surrounded by white accordion gates.

And as the ref stands in front of us, I see Hola's rear end twitch, as though she wants to break her sit. Even as I remind her, "Hola, sit!" I know we've got trouble.

There's a suggestion in the CGC *Evaluator Guide* that the ref give some general introductory remarks, such as that dogs are not required to perform with the precision required in formal obedience. This is something that I'm sure does not even occur to most people, who have never seen a formal obedience competition. TV tends to show only the conformation beauty pageants, not so-called performance events such as Agility and Obedience.

But above all, the guide says, "The Canine Good Citizen experience should be fun for the handler and the dog."

Then, there is your life.

"Are you ready?" asks the ref.

"Yes," I say, and she nods—the signal to begin.

Hola starts in a solid sit, but her mind keeps trying to play an inner game on her, telling her the ref needs a good greeting, maybe one with both paws on her tummy.

I keep still, my body at right angles to the mat and my eyes drilled into our evaluator. She's looking at me, not the dog, because she wants us to pass. Most dogs will not jump on a person who does not make eye contact with them.

The ref comes up to me and shakes my hand, and in my peripheral vision I see Hola with her head up, trying to dominate her instincts as they circle one another. The ref steps back, and Hola sticks her sit.

She's just passed item #1, "Accepting a friendly stranger."

"May I pet your dog?" asks the ref.

I'd like to say no.

And, in fact, the guidelines to item #2, "Sitting politely for petting," require neither the formal question nor any particular answer from the handler.

"Yes."

And she bends over and pets Hola.

Now, Hola never had any problem with shyness, so she's not going to bark, flinch, or bite—all unacceptable reactions—but I know there's a finely calibrated jab-and-counter going on in her mind as she tries to keep four paws on the floor and her exuberance contained for the exercise, even as her old self fires back with a flurry of good reasons to jump up.

Despite the item's name, the guide says that the dog is allowed to stand to receive petting (the Volhards' CGC book gets this wrong). Hola stands, and the ref says, "It's okay; she just can't jump all over me."

Now that, says a part of Hola I know too well, *sounds like a good idea.*

The ref's hand loiters as it glides through Hola's fur, burying fingers in a weave of Bernese warmth, and I can tell Hola is working her usual voodoo on the human spirit. Then the ref bends over Hola and lifts up her front paws, peeks into her ears, and pulls back her lips.

She steps away, saying, "Thank you."

Hola has passed items #2 and #3, "Appearance and grooming."

"That's a beautiful girl," says the ref, breaking her professional detachment for a moment. "What a doll."

But I'm troubled by an almost imperceptible tug on the leash as the old Hola warns me she may be the underdog here, but she's got a few variations left in her bag.

There's a saying in the sweet science: punch a boxer and box a puncher.

Now, Hola is not a boxer, but she certainly has a lot of punch as we enter into the brutal middle rounds, the items that can make or break a dog's confidence as they pile one upon another in a flurry of evaluations that can, given a shaky move early on, take on the inevitability of a dirge.

"Okay," says the ref, stepping back into the center of the ring. "Walking on a loose lead. Keep her in control here. Go around that column. Okay, turn left. Go straight. Make a right. Around that column. Good. Keep it loose . . . Good."

While the ref talks, I ramp up a sotto voce barrage of encouragement, more to get Hola's eyes on me than to tell her what to do: "Hola baby, over here, with me, with me, heel, heel, over here, with me . . ."

The litany of the amateur in the evaluation ring.

Suddenly five or six of the people from the audience come into the ring and start wandering around, chatting and acting crazy. I'm not sure where the tradition came from, but most of the CGC tests I've seen inspire someone in the "crowd" for item #5, "Walking through a crowd," to act as though they're drunk.

Usually, they'll sing.

In all my years as a drunk walking among drunks in a drunken state, while I saw many people crying, I never once saw a person break into song. Perhaps I needed to broaden my acquaintance.

The phony drunk doesn't distract Hola, but she does distract me.

And bad Hola—the one that's been waiting at ringside—sees an opening: she comes out of her corner with tremendous speed and power, unfurling a body punch from the depths of a cavern of steel, as she rockets a jib-jab at me and suddenly flies to the end of the leash, taking out the slack.

Then she leans back into her powerful rear pistons, gathering leverage for an explosion through the air onto the back of the "drunk," who is actually her old teacher Wendy from her Family Manners Skills class.

Staying cool, I say, "Good girl!" which may seem like a strange reaction. But it works; in the real world, most of the time this phrase is followed by some lavish praise and sometimes even a little treat. I don't have any treats in the test ring, but it's my emergency mantra, the one that always gets her attention.

Hola comes back to me, beating down the sneak attack, and looks up with a big smile, waiting for her reward.

"Good girl!" I say.

We'd almost failed—if she'd jumped up on Wendy, she'd have been disqualified—but we didn't.

Ding.

Onward.

Hola is still in this thing, with a bell.

.   .   .

"Thank you, crowd," says the ref, dismissing them, and she directs me and Hola over to the corner of the ring farthest from the entrance to the club.

"Okay, we're going to do some basic obedience exercises now," she says. "Ask your dog to sit. Okay. Now down."

"Down," I say to a nicely seated Hola. She looks at me vacantly.

"Down!" I say again, raising my hand over her head, our signal.

Again, nothing.

It looks like Hola's old instincts, having punked out in the clinch earlier, have decided to make it a game of attrition— wearing out my new, improved dog gradually, item by item, grinding down her poise, waiting for the strength to leave her paws, confusing her with a dogged persistence, and now: Hola seems stunned.

The ref watches us carefully, and I can see the other handlers, our friends from the classes, start to lean forward, probably thinking, *What a silly exercise to fail*. If you're gonna go down in the CGC, don't do it on the down. It's too common.

Faith descends in that moment. Hola's too strong to let her dark side—which I am beginning to think of as the Bad Dog—win on a walk. I will her to listen to my heart racing hard in her direction.

"Hola," I whisper. "With me, now." I breathe, matching her breath; the ringside recedes, the ref dissolves into the mat.

"Hola baby," I say, "do it for Mommy now. Down."

She goes down.

"Okay," says the ref. "Ask your dog to stay."

"Hola, stay!" with the hand signal: flat palm, fingers down, two inches in front of her nose.

"Turn around and go back ten steps. Okay. Now go back to your dog."

I'm not afraid of Hola's stay: even on her worst days, when she had pounded herself with a hailstorm of doubt, her stay was pretty solid.

"Now leave her in a sit or a down, whichever you prefer, and go back five steps. Turn around. Okay." A quiet moment: my favorite in the test. What's coming is incredible. "Now ask your dog to come."

Spreading my arms and leaning back, I say, "Hola, come!"

Her recalls are always comical: she explodes out of her stay, running toward me with such thunderous enthusiasm, often banging into me at the end with so much gusto I fall over. It's not the most nuanced recall in the world.

But, hey, I think, as I'm snapping on her leash after recovering my balance, she just passed items #6 and #7, "Sit and down on command" and "Coming when called."

Just so does the enemy soften us with complacency; the Bad Dog is a master of the distance game.

Looking back, I should have anticipated that our opponent would again hunt down a weakness where we didn't think we had one. Because the next item, #8, "Reaction to another dog," was not one we'd worried about.

In it, the handler and the ref both have a dog they ask to sit while they shake hands and go on their way; throughout the exercise, there are two humans standing between the dogs, who are not supposed to rush over to one another, bark, play-bow, or otherwise act like normal dogs.

Hola had been knocking it out of the park during training, sitting like a little Buddha to my left as I shook hands with my classmates and we moved along.

The ref, who had stepped out of the ring for a moment,

returns leading her shi tzu, Molly, who looks like ten pounds of trouble to me: she has a big pink bow all but buried in her salon-shiny white fur, and, worse, she is just the kind of pint-sized pretty girl Hola adores.

Placing Molly gently on the ground to her left, the ref says, "Okay, now let's walk past each other once."

As Hola and I go past them, I can see the fire-red eyes of the Bad Dog gleaming out of Hola's as she gets a whiff of this dog she's never seen before. Too late, I realize that Hola isn't really able to sit quietly until she's familiar with a dog: first time out, she always jumps on them.

We about-turn and the ref says, "Come up to me and have your dog sit. Then I'll shake your hand. Ready?"

Nope, nada, niente, I'm thinking as I nod.

"Let's go."

In a moment, we're side by side and I ask Hola to sit. She does. I turn to the ref and—

There's a rifle shot of black fur screaming past me below, and I see the ref lose her balance, catching herself with a shuffle, and Hola squeaks left-right-left with electrifying speed, driving her nose into the shi tzu's face and stick-pinning her with a paw half-nelson . . . It all happens so fast, between beats of my heart, I am not even conscious of stepping back and pulling Hola into a heel at my side, saying, *"Hola, back! Stop! Heel! No!"*—nearly every one-syllable dog word I know.

After I reel Hola in, the ref smiles sympathetically and says, "Let's try that one again. She was a little nervous."

It's a well-kept secret, but the AKC's guidelines allow the evaluator to let a dog try a single item again if she fails. So our ref is by the book as she lets us do another about-turn and come back toward her. What she can't do is convince me we have a chance here.

Hola has failed.

There is no scenario I can envision where she succeeds in sticking her sit with that new best friend she doesn't know just inches away from her nose—not one.

Deep in myself, I feel a tragic melancholy rise, like a man who's walked all the way across America to find California in ruins.

But Hola, as usual, isn't listening to me.

Standing farther away from the ref and her shi tzu this time, I say, "Hola, sit."

I'm looking into her eyes now, both of them, saying over and over, "Hola, sit, good, sit, stay, good," a mishmash of calmly spoken commands that don't convey much except stay where you are and just ignore my hand gliding out, groping the air for the ref's hand, making contact, waiting for her release to go on, and as she says, "Okay," I move briskly forward off my left leg, getting Hola as far as possible from the shi tzu as quickly as I can.

She cranes her neck around, a wistful final glance, and I let my shoulders drop and look down at my hands: I'm holding the leash so tightly that my knuckles are white.

THE REF POINTS to a woman in a blue blazer sitting in a brown metal folding chair by the fire extinguisher.

"We're going to have you go out of sight for three minutes," she says. "Give Meryl here your leash and go through the doors over there. I'll call you back when—"

"What about number nine," I say. "The distractions."

"We did it already," says the ref.

"What?"

Item #9, "Reaction to distraction," requires the dog to remain calm during distractions such as dropped crutches, joggers, wheelchairs, whatever.

"During the walk through the crowd," she says, "didn't you hear it? We dropped a lot of stuff."

"Oh."

I hadn't noticed anything—our focus was just that intense.

As directed, I ask the woman in the blazer, "Will you hold my dog, please?"

"Yes, of course."

"I'll be right back."

"Let me guess, in three minutes?"

Everyone's a comedian.

Here we are already: item #10—our bête noire, our Waterloo: "Supervised separation."

As I'm leaving the ring, going out through the swinging doors into the vestibule that leads to the parking lot, I stand up against the wall and pray not to hear Hola whining, crying, yelping, screeching, yowling, or doing any of the things she's not supposed to do.

It occurs to me this is the most spiritual of all the CGC test items. There is nothing I can do now. Hola passes the test or she doesn't.

I just have to let go of her, think happy thoughts, wish her a protective paw against the attractions of her former self, rely on all the training we have done.

I need to have a little faith.

Leaving the Ring

AFTER HOLA PASSES HER CGC TEST, I immediately send a note to Susan Conant. She has become a pen pal during this process, and I attach a picture I'd taken with my cell phone of some of her books I'd seen stacked on a table near the Port Chester entrance before we took the test. "It seemed to me like a good omen," I tell her.

She replies immediately: "Oh, Marty, I am so proud of you and Hola! I like to imagine that the copies of my books contributed to the ambience that helped Hola to be such a good girl."

And I call my sister; and my friend Clark, who's still in rehab; and my new sponsor, Darryl, who isn't. And I write a note to Mary Burch, showing off, which is strongly encouraged in the dog world.

And then I call Gloria. She doesn't answer. I leave a message. Then I saddle up Hola and take her out into the blizzard to celebrate.

There is nothing Hola likes more than snow. It's the environment where she makes the most sense. I like to think that on a genetic level it's like one of us humans going back to the town we grew up in; suddenly, we are home. We can relax.

So she's bounding through the drifts piling up in front of

our building, doing backflips as though trying to spring off the wind, and I almost don't feel my phone vibrating in my pocket.

It's Gloria.

"Hey," I say, breathing hard into the phone. "You'll never guess—"

"She passed?"

"Yup, she passed. Didn't whine at all in number ten. Had some problems with the, you know, ignoring the other dog one, but she made it up. It was amazing. It's like she knew how important it was."

"Wow."

"You're surprised?"

"Amazed," she says. "I wanted to go but the snow—it was too dangerous. You guys worked so hard. Probably no one worked harder for a CGC than you did. Maybe ever."

"Probably."

"Where are you? Outside?"

"Yeah. Hola's making snow angels. They look like . . . uh, kind of like her."

Wind tears down the street, slamming into the snow, and I turn my back toward it.

"Oh, my God," I say, "this is quite a freaking storm."

"I know," Gloria says. "I can see you."

"What's it like in—what? What did you say?"

"I can see you. Turn around."

Just then, Hola decides to use her daddy as a pivot around which to test the maximum centrifugal energy generation possible by a Bernese mountain dog, and she rockets around me, twisting me up in the leash just as I'm trying to turn.

I stagger back and, feet clamped in the leash, tumble into the snow.

Hola stands over me, panting, and I swear I can see her trying not to laugh.

"Ha, ha," I say to her. "Ha, ha, ha."

You're welcome, she says.

So I'm sitting up, wiping off my glasses and digging for my phone in the snow when I see a familiar pair of L. L. Bean duck boots and then a familiar red coat and hat, and Gloria reaches her hand down and tries to pull me up.

Except I'm heavier than she is, and the ground is soft and icy, and she falls down on top of me, and we're lying there in the snow together trying to catch our breath.

Which gets harder when Hola decides to jump on top of both of us for a Bernese family reunion.

A WEEK LATER, a Saturday morning after some of the snow has melted, I'm sitting on the bed with my coffee and the animals, trying to explain to Gloria why Ruby the cat likes me.

"It's because I accept her as she is," I say. "I don't judge her like you do."

"I don't judge Ruby," Gloria says.

"Do you think she's fat?"

"Yes."

"Do you think she's cranky?"

"Yes."

"What about her personality? How would you characterize that?"

"Bad."

"Are these positive qualities you just said?"

"Not really."

"So you're judging Ruby."

"Yes," she admits, "but she's too stupid to know that."

"Shhh," I say, "she's right there. She can hear you."

Ruby scampers into the back room, where Gloria keeps her upright piano and her library of cookbooks and American standards of the songwriting art, and in a few seconds we hear three clear notes from the keyboard. The rhythm is off, but it sounds to me a lot like a song I recognize.

"You hear that?" I ask Gloria.

"Kitten on the Keys?"

"No," I say. "It sounded like the first three notes of that Pat Benatar song."

"You're crazy."

" 'Love Is a Battlefield.' "

At that moment, there's a knock on the door, and it turns out to be Jesus the doorman with a package for me. It's from Mary Burch, head of the Canine Good Citizen program: a signed copy of her new book *Citizen Canine,* the first AKC-sanctioned training guide for the CGC. Her note thanks me for my commitment to the test—which is, as you know, almost epic.

There's also a bond-weight envelope embossed with a gold AKC seal marked "*For Hola.*" Inside is a card congratulating her on her certification and an Olympic-size gold medal with a festive yellow-and-blue neck ribbon.

Respectfully, I hang it around Hola's neck.

She stands there, bewildered, as she usually does when odd things like hats and sweaters are forced onto her head by ridiculous people. Her usual reaction is to shrug it off within seconds, then check for yumminess. But not this time.

Shock turns to a kind of quiet pride as she sits confidently, beaming, as though waiting for the press conference to start.